© 2015 by Leon Capetanos

First Edition, 2015
All Rights Reserved
Library of Congress Cataloging-in-Publication Data

Capetanos, Leon.
The Time Box —1st ed.
p. cm.
ISBN: 978-0-9911211-8-2
2015944898

Owl Canyon Press
Boulder, Colorado

THE TIME BOX

LEON CAPETANOS

OWL CANYON PRESS

For Chloë, John and Lisa

Nothing you can know that isn't known
Nothing you can see that isn't shown
Nowhere you can be that isn't where you're meant to be
It's easy
All you need is love

John Lennon

CHAPTER ONE

I HAD A DREAM the other night. I was floating out among the stars and planets. I didn't have on a space suit so far as I could tell. I was just floating, freer and lighter than when I'm in the water. I felt there were others with me but I couldn't see them because they were behind me. I could hear some whispers and a couple of laughs. I wasn't scared. I was enjoying myself. I did a flip turn and then I could look back at the Earth. It was beautiful and the bright moon was over it. Then I noticed that I was speeding away from it. The Earth was getting smaller and smaller. I suddenly wondered where was I going? And just as I was getting queasy from the question in my head, I woke up.

My name is Thomas Adkins Johnson. You can call me Tommy. Adkins is my mother Claire's last name before she got married. My dad is Rick Stanley Johnson. I'm twelve years old but I turn thirteen in about a week. I can't wait to be thirteen. I'll be a real teenager then. Being what people call a "tween" is the worst. You're just in some kind of holding pattern, or what Catholics like my friend Mignon call purgatory.

As you may or may not know, Johnson is the second most popular last name in the USA. That's after Smith, which, of course, is number one. Go look in your local phone book (if you can find one) and see how many Johnsons there are. Even in my small city, there are pages and pages of Johnsons and quite a few Thomas or Tom or Tommy or Tommi or T Johnsons. Get on Facebook. See how that works out. Seven hundred thousand so far for Tommy J. So I have an ordinary name and it makes me feel kind of ordinary. Because of my initials, some of my friends (basically Kareem) call me Taj, which I kind of like.

I envy people with unique names. One of my good friends is Micky Boonaling. His mother and father are from Thailand. Micky's a math whiz and really a silly, nice person. Just think. They are the only Boonalings in our phone book. Another friend of mine is Maria Papadopoulos. Her family has a restaurant downtown, The Acropolis. They probably never get the wrong mail or the wrong phone calls or emails. She says in Greece Papadopoulos isn't a rare name, but it is here. My friend Kareem has a normal last name, Brooks, but he has a cool first name, which means "generous" in Arabic, or so he told me.

Some people have really interesting names. My favorite was a girl who was born on an airplane going to Germany, where her dad was in the army. Lufthansa Jenkins. We were friends in the fourth grade. I called her Lufti. My other good friends are: David Ryan, who has red hair and is a real prankster; Jacob Meyer, who knows some serious jokes; and Mignon Eubanks who I mentioned before. She's a girl. You might say she's my *girlfriend*, but in a casual way. (At least that's the way it was.)

Mignon is a unique name. The only "mignon" I ever heard of was on the menu at Sullivan's Steak House: filet mignon. Turns out (well, I looked it up on the Internet), "mignon" in French means "cute" or "nice" or "delicate." And she's sort of that. She has delicate features I'd say, grey-blue eyes and pale skin. Her hair is black as a crow's feathers. She's nice but on the soccer field she's a real competitor and she's not delicate there.

Once Mignon told me she thinks she has African blood somewhere in her past generations. Her family's originally from Louisiana, and she says most people down there have a drop of African in their DNA. Speaking of this, my friend Kareem is an African American, but to be honest, I don't like that term, "African American." It just seems so long and clumsy. Say it: "African American." It's so fancy, so ooh la la. Too stiff. Doesn't match somehow. One day Kareem and I agreed on this. So we invented a new way of saying it quickly. Double A, like the batteries. So if we're describing somebody—like the new guy, Lawrence Jennings—we say, Lawrence is a stocky Double A guy. That's how we use it.

Anyway, all this is beside the facts of the story I need to tell. This whole year has been full of important events and what teachers call "challenges." Good and bad challenges.

They can be sad or happy or a mixture of both.

∎

I guess I should describe myself. I have sandy brown hair and blue eyes like my mother. I'm about a normal height for my age and I'm not fat or skinny. Almost everything about me seems average. I'm not great at sports. I did play some football last fall but I was a reserve in the line. This year I found a sport I really liked: cross country. I couldn't play football this year, because they share the same season.

I'm not the fastest on my team, but I do have endurance, especially running in the woods or over the hillsides. I don't think I would have the same endurance if I was running around on the track, round and round like a hamster in a wheel. I usually finish in the middle of the pack with my team. My times are getting better, which keeps me positive for practice. (I don't want to be huffing at the rear.) But what I really like is the feeling you have, running out in nature. You feel like you're getting somewhere, traveling, and that the air you're breathing is sweeter somehow. The light is always changing through the leaves and the moving clouds. You hear the birds singing and the squirrels dashing through the brush. And you have time to think about stuff in your life, which I have been doing more and more of these last months. Some days I run on my own down a greenway along the creek near my house. There are a few regulars on the greenway. An old man on a big bike. A large woman who jogs in a trash bag. A couple walking their little dog.

Anyway, there's always baseball in the spring. Coach Wrenn says I have good hand-eye coordination, which seems to be essential in baseball. The main thing is I like baseball. The grass. The smack of the ball in your glove. So that's a little summary.

Of course, things change all the time. Last year, in sixth grade, I only thought about regular stuff: school and vacations, sports and gaming and what girl I liked, etcetera. But this year that all changed. The change started with a fall field trip to Chapel Hill, the home of the University of North Carolina. The Tar Heels are my favorite team. Mignon pulls for Duke, but I think she does that just to annoy me.

■

The idea of the field trip was for my seventh-grade class to see a show at the Morehead Planetarium: "The Universe Is Your Home." I didn't think much about it. It was just a good chance to get out with my friends and goof around a little.

The theater of the planetarium is a big, dark room with a strange machine in the middle. When we took our seats, Mignon was on my right and Kareem was on my left. Micky sat behind me, kicking my chair, until Miss Robbins told him to stop. When he didn't, she moved him two rows away. We didn't know what to expect. We were just happy to be out of school. Kareem said if the lights went out, he was going to take a nap. (I can't nap. Even in elementary school I couldn't. Something would always distract me: a bug on the window; Susie Jenkins, smacking her lips; Sid Flack, farting.) Anyway, I was relaxing in this comfortable chair, just like at the movies, when the lights dimmed and the program started.

What I remember from that point on is a crazy jumble. Some things that the moderator said stunned my brain and then sent my mind flying off in all directions. The show started with our solar system—those planets that we're familiar with. David asked a question about Uranus to get a cheap laugh. But the laughing stopped real quick when the guy leading the show said that the sun is more than 95 million miles away from us, That's lucky for us. Any closer and we'd be burning up. Any farther away and we'd be shivering, or just plain frozen.

Then he started talking about our "neighborhood," which is the Milky Way, our galaxy. Pretty big neighborhood, because he said—this I remember clearly—that it's 120,000 light years across. Light years? He began to explain a light year, and I sort of had an idea about that: something that for one year was moving at the speed of light (including light itself), and that's fast. 186,000 miles per second. (Who clocked it?) Well, something traveling at that speed would take 120,000 years to get across the Milky Way.

My head stung. I shook it. Then he said something that made it worse. There are billions of stars in our galaxy, our nice "neighborhood." So many stars that they couldn't get a sure count—200, maybe 400 billion. At first, I thought he said a million, but it was a billion, and then I started feeling kind of dizzy with the stars revolving above in the dark. Of course, our sun is just one of the billions of stars, and kind of an ordinary one.

Now Kareem wasn't napping. He had a puzzled look

on his face, and when I looked over to Mignon, she gave me a left eyebrow lift, which sort of asked me if I was okay. I nodded but it was a lie. So there I am, still thinking of that giant galaxy and trying to get my head around it and how big it was. And then somewhere that voice was still talking, saying that the stars we see in the night sky are basically 5,000 light years away, but that if we had a good telescope we could see things in the universe that are really distant. He mentioned something called a quasar, which is millions, even billions, of light years away from the Milky Way.

I think my brain had a short circuit then and that blew my mental fuse. I sat there staring up into space when Mignon leaned over. "Why are you breathing so hard?" she asked.

"Was I?"

She nodded.

"Just thinking." And that was the truth.

The guy talking, a professor I'm sure, seemed happy about these numbers and the size of the universe and the distance from the quasars. He wanted to show us what a nice neighborhood we were living in and how comfortable the Milky Way is in the "vastness" of the universe. All I could think about was that cold dark sky and the blinking stars with light that had travelled thousands of years just to reach me in my backyard. Those stars could already be dead and all that's left would be the twinkling. By the time the last light reaches us here, we'll be long gone, for sure.

That show changed the way I looked at the sky forever.

CHAPTER TWO

O**N THE WAY BACK**, bouncing in the bus, Mignon was chirpy as ever. She was talking about maybe going skiing in the mountains this winter.

"I never learned to ski. Waterskiing, yes, but snow skiing, that was out of the question. When we lived in Baton Rouge, I didn't ever think about snow. Do you ski?" she asked, looking at me with her head cocked to one side.

I nodded cool like. "I've been skiing twice, up near Boone. Then another time, up in West Virginia. It's fun when you get the hang of it."

I remembered pretty clearly the tow line when I was learning. I remembered the girl trying to get me to snow plow. "French fries...pizza...French fries...pizza." I must've fallen a hundred times. I even got run over once by an out-of-control blind woman who'd been taken up on the slope for an outing. She lost her minder and came swishing down the hill, singing all the time what seemed like an old spiritual. The one word I could make out was

"Jesus," right before she clipped me. I didn't get hurt and neither did she. She fell on her right side, slid about another ten yards, and kept singing until her minder came up apologizing. She seemed thrilled, even in her darkness, smiling from the feeling she'd just experienced.

"You think I could get the hang of it?" Mignon asked.

"Of course. You're an athlete," I said.

The conversation paused. Kareem leaned over the seat. "You got the homework assignment for English?"

"Yeah," I answered.

"Text me with it when you get home," Kareem said.

I nodded and then Kareem leaned even closer. "That star crap nearly blew my mind," he whispered, pulling his hoodie over his big head. So I wasn't alone.

Another pause. Cars zipping by on the highway. Somebody had music on in the back of the bus. Must have been David, because it was bad hip-hop. I was thinking of that picture of the galaxy, like a saucer or a Frisbee. The swirl of it.

"What's wrong with you today?" Mignon asked, giving me a punch.

"What do you mean?"

"You seem like you're not here. Like you're depressed or something."

"I'm in the Milky Way."

"So, aren't we all?" she said, looking at the cracked blue polish on her toe nails.

I tried to get my mind off the universe, playing Dumbbell on my phone. My phone is too old to get really good games on it. It belonged to my Mom first. Mignon has an iPhone. A nice one. One of these days, maybe.

Anyway, we got back to school, packed up, and Mignon and I headed for home. We lived close together. If it had been raining we might have hopped a bus or somebody's mom would have given us a lift, but most days we'd walk. It takes about thirty minutes for us to get home. Kareem would usually walk with us, carrying his basketball or dribbling it or we would pass it back and forth. But lately Kareem, once we got to the park, would peel off and head to the basketball court to play with some older guys. He was a good friend, but I knew he was drifting away. He'd grown a good six inches since last year and was above six feet now. The doctor had told him he would grow to about six feet eight before he was done. He loved basketball anyway, but this news made him get serious. He started practicing whenever he could, and he kept getting better and better. He was the best player in the seventh grade by a long shot. So I knew he'd hang with the ball players more and more, and that was okay. That was his future. He was lucky that he knew what his future was going to be. I sure didn't have an idea. I didn't know whether I was really good at anything, except maybe imagining.

"See you guys later." Kareem gave a wave and trotted toward the game that had already started. Me and Mignon walked on without talking for a while.

"You still thinking about the planetarium stuff?" she asked.

"Yeah. Aren't you?"

"No."

"How can you not?" I asked.

"I think it's interesting, but I got a test tomorrow. And it's not on the stars or the Milky Way."

"Me, too."

"Then we should do a little studying. At least I should."

"What does that mean?" I asked.

"It means you're smart and you can read something once and it stays in your head. I have to go over stuff again and again."

"You're smart, too," I said. And I wasn't kidding.

"Sometimes I wonder."

I looked up at the sky. Puffy clouds drifting by. The sun—our star, our personal star—going lower behind the big trees. Gold light was on Mignon's face when I looked back at her. She punched me again on the shoulder.

"Stop it. I don't like that dreamy look on your face."

"Okay! Park later?"

"Maybe after dinner," she said.

"I'll be better," I promised her.

"But all the stars will be out. You'll get depressed."

"Not depressed. Just worried."

"See ya."

She took the turn towards her house and I trotted home. Yes, I was still in the Milky Way but my eyes were on her and I shivered when she looked back at me and waved. It wasn't from the cold. Maybe she was beaming me with some super thought waves. (Like Professor X) That would be wild. It's funny how two people can go through the same experience and see it in completely different ways. That planetarium show scared me. That's the truth. It made me think how insignificant I am, or should I say, we are. Mignon saw it as some great reality, or at least evidence that a powerful and, as they say about the Grand Canyon, "awe-inspiring" god was out there making it happen. In time, after we both deal with it, I'm sure we'll come closer together on this subject. She'll get a little scared and I'll get a little awed. They're almost the same thing.

CHAPTER THREE

NOW I NEED to tell you about my parents. They're part of the story and you need to know them from the get-go.

My dad is a senior service technician at Langley BMW, one of the biggest BMW dealers in the Southeast. He's been working there for about twelve years. They tried to put him in an office about two years ago but he said no. He likes being in the garage and dealing with machinery better than dealing with complaining people and what he calls "politics." He's always loved cars and engines. He told me the first time he broke down an engine was with his dad, when he was fourteen. It was a Fiat 124 Coupe. Anyway, my dad is usually in a good mood. If something makes him mad, his ears turn red and he'll stomp around some and maybe use a good curse word once in a while but I've never seen him break anything on purpose. We have the same sandy colored hair, but he cuts his real short. I let mine grown a little shaggy until Mom drags me to Great Clips.

Mom is kind of blonde and, even if I say so myself, she's very pretty. Mom and Dad knew each other in high school, but they didn't date then. They moved in different circles, they say. They joke about it. Mom went to college while Dad was in the Army. A few days after he got out of the Army, they met in the grocery store, right by the apples. Then they started going out. As Mom tells it, her dad didn't like the fact that she was going out with a guy just out of the Army with no college degree. Her dad was a college professor of history and he thought that it would be a bad match. But Dad was good-looking and fun-loving, as well as handy. Mom likes handy. They were going to the movies in her car one night and it broke down. Dad jumped out and fixed whatever it was with his Swiss army knife while Mom held a flashlight for him. She said that was the moment she may have fallen in love. As for Dad, he said he fell for her right by the apples. He didn't know how to talk to her when he was in high school but after being overseas, he wasn't scared of talking to a girl—any girl. So when they have an anniversary there's always something relating to apples that they give each other. I guess that's cute.

Mom works too. Part-time. She's real busy during tax season doing people's income taxes for them. She has about thirty people she works for every year. She calls the money she makes the college fund.

One of her majors in college was math. I don't have her math skills, of course, but maybe my sister, Ella, does. She's nine and she's a real character. More blonde than my mother and tough as horseshoe nails. She's never still, moving around even when she's doing homework. She likes sports more than me and I think she wants to keep playing soccer all year long. We both like to read and she's gotten Dad to read a few books to her. I think she's trying to educate him. We get along real well. She thinks I'm funny and I think she's funny, too. She kids me about Mignon and I don't mind, because sometimes she says what I'm feeling about her without me having to say it.

Anyway, we also have a dog that Mom got from the pound. His name is Jake. He's small but really brave. Mom thinks he's some kind of terrier. He keeps the squirrels in our yard jumping. One day he's gonna catch one.

So that's the family unit. Dad's parents moved to Sanibel Island, Florida, three years ago. We don't see them much anymore. Mom's Dad is living up in the mountains and still teaching at a small college. He moved there after my grandmother died. That must have been seven years ago. He doesn't visit anymore. Mom thinks he still misses Ada, his wife, my grandma. We communicate with all of them on the computer. On Dad's side there's his brother, Aaron, and his family, over in Greensboro, and Mom's brother and sister live in Dallas, Texas, now.

As for our vehicles, Mom drives a Honda Odyssey. Dad uses his Ford 150 truck almost every day. It has 98, 000 miles on it. Should hit 100,000 pretty quick. He also keeps his baby in the garage: a 1996 BMW 530 with manual shift that he bought from a customer. He took care of that car for years and when the lady that owned it wanted to sell it or trade it, he snatched it up. Also in the garage, aside from Ella's and my bikes, are the pieces of an old Norton motorcycle that my Dad's trying to put back together. My mom hopes he never will. Mom loves to garden and bake. She makes great meatloaf and some awesome lasagna. There's nothing she can't cook. On special days she'll make a roast or a big pot of stew, especially in the winter when Dad's friends bring home some venison. In the summer, we eat a lot of fish: some that Dad's caught and some that I've hooked at Lake Waverly.

Mom's always hugging me and Ella. She gives us a good squeeze most every day. We make fun of her sometimes and act like we're running away from her squeezing. But she catches us every time and we're so glad she does. Dad's not much of a hugger. He might give you a pat on the back. He thinks I'm a genius, because I get good grades.

One Sunday afternoon, when he was messing with the Norton, he started talking to me about that. "You must have your mother's brains," he said. "I wasn't much good at school, except in a few subjects. I liked working in shop class. That's where I felt comfortable. Sometimes I think I could have played less and studied harder, but even then, I don't think I would've been as good at my studies as you are, well, kind of naturally."

He tousled my hair. "Don't look so serious, Thomas." He calls me Thomas sometimes—I think because it amuses him.

"That's why I went in the Army. It seemed like that was the best thing to do. Aaron was in college in Virginia. It was expensive, but he had the brains to take advantage of it. I couldn't see Dad having to keep the two of us in college at the same time. Maybe that was an excuse. But the Army told me they'd help with college after I served. In fact, they did. I went to Wake Community for a year and was doing good. But I really needed a job what with being married, baby on the way." He pointed at me with a wink.

"So I got hired at Langley VW and after a while they moved me over to the BMW shop. Anyway, I always knew, from early, that I wanted to work on cars—engines, transmissions, whatever. I had a talent for it from as early I can remember. Mechanical things came easy to me. I could fix a clock or a sump pump or an ancient outboard. I figured I had a gift and I still feel lucky about it. Everybody has some kind of gift and the lucky ones see it early and it fills them up. I'm happy working on this old motorcycle, which I will probably only ride a couple of times before your mother makes me sell it. So then, I'll get another thing to work on. An old car or tractor—something." He paused, wiping his hands on a dark rag.

"Well, I haven't found my talent yet," I said.

"You will if you just don't get caught up in what other people expect you to do."

I think this was the longest conversation I ever had with my dad.

■

Mom made her special spaghetti sauce that night after the planetarium trip. I'd finished my homework before dinner, so after I ate, I grabbed my bike and rode down to the park. Johnny Shelton was there with another guy. They were smoking and laughing over by the basketball court. Johnny was a high school guy, always in trouble at school or with the local cops over this or that. He was always friendly to me. After about fifteen minutes Mignon rode up on her bike.

"Lot of stars out tonight," she said.

"Yeah."

I hadn't looked but now that she mentioned it, I rolled back on the picnic table and stared straight up. The sky was so clear down here in the park. Mignon sat on the bench.

"I've been thinking about what you said. How small we are and how big the universe is." She was staring straight up at the sky.

"And we don't really know how big it is. We're still trying to figure it out."

"Maybe that's what you should study when you go to college," she said looking back to me.

"Who says I'm going to college?"

"Me."

"Well, I think it would be frustrating to just think about that all the time. It could drive you loony."

"It's kind of wonderful, too."

"How so?"

"Don't you believe in God?" she asked.

"Sort of."

"What does that mean?"

"It means that sometimes I wonder with all the craziness and disaster stuff going on in the world, the diseases and massacres and people starving, I wonder if there even is a god, whether he cares about us at all."

"Shut up. Lightning could hit you," she laughed as she rolled back on the table next to me.

"Not much lightning this time of year."

"And what about Jesus?" she asked.

"We all love Jesus." I was trying to be sarcastic.

"You go to church, don't you?"

"Not every Sunday. But most every Sunday."

"Do you pray?" she asked, looking straight at me.

"Every now and then." I tried to remember the last time I really prayed.

"I pray every morning and every night."

"What do you pray for?"

"I don't pray 'for' anything." She was scolding me. "I'm just thankful to be alive in this great, beautiful world and universe. And sometimes I pray for people who are suffering."

She paused and I stopped looking at the stars. I wanted to see her face. Now she was staring up at the sky. "Is that the Big Dipper?" she asked.

"It could be." I stretched up. I liked to act like I knew a lot about it. "Yeah, and that bright star there is the North Star. It's pretty close, sort of. But the guy at the planetarium said that the North Star we see—that light—started out in about the year 1580."

"Gosh. That doesn't seem close to me."

"See what I mean?" I was trying to make a point.

Suddenly she bolted up and grabbed my sleeve.

"There's a shooting star. Did you see it?"

"Missed it. But you know it's not a star. It's a meteor."

"Thanks." I think she was being sarcastic.

"Sorry," I said.

She stared up at the sky again. "'Twinkle, twinkle, little star or meteor, how I wonder what you are.'"

When I'd look up I could feel her looking at me. When I would look back at her, she would turn her face to the stars again. We were so close to each other I could hear her breathing. It went on that way for a long time. We didn't talk. I could hear cars on Glenwood. I could hear a few birds in the trees. A dog was barking in the distance. It sounded like Rusty, a big old German shepherd that Mister Spears owned. Then, finally, after being silent and after all the stargazing, we ended up turning face to face, looking straight at each other. Now I could feel her breath. My heart started beating real fast. Suddenly Mignon jumped up off the table and picked up her bike.

"Later," she said, and pedaled away fast.

I watched her until she reached the street light and then I sat up. The Murphys' dogs were howling like they did almost every night around bed time. Rusty had stopped barking. I waited for my heart to calm down. It was a great moon tonight. I could see the craters. It looked so close, like it was just beyond the railroad tracks. But it was Mignon's close-up face that stuck with me as I rode home up Park Drive. For whatever reason, the universe seemed even bigger that night. Or was I getting smaller?

CHAPTER FOUR

ALL THIS THINKING continued for days and days. I don't mean every minute, but all I would have to do is look up at the sky and think back to all the distances and the endless darkness. The empty and silent space. Mignon was the only person who knew how I was stressing out about this information. She tried to distract me and in her case that was easy.

"Don't dwell on it," she said.

"I don't dwell on it. Occasionally it comes up in my mind."

"It's nice today. The leaves are turning. It's so pretty. Think about that."

She was right. Red leaves on the dogwoods and maples. Yellow on the oak. That also meant I'd be raking soon. I took a deep breath of the crisp air. Nitrogen and oxygen and other stuff.

"What are you doing this weekend?" I asked.

"Jeannie and I are going to the mall on Saturday. Maybe we'll see a movie. You should come."

"I don't know. I got yard work to do. What time are you going?"

"Around twelve."

I just nodded, but I really wanted to go, even with that annoying little Jeannie tagging along. She never shuts up, always making comments about other people. So the idea of a mall hangout with Mignon took over my brain. Then I made the mistake of mentioning it to Micky, who said he'd like to hang, too. That would be a problem, because Jeannie thinks Micky's weird and she might mess things up. But she likes Kareem a lot, so I asked him what was up for Saturday, but Kareem was going to play b-ball at the Y, but Micky told David, who said he could come later. Things get very complicated very quickly, and then, when things don't match up, everybody bails. It's exhausting.

That Saturday, Mom drove me over to the mall and Micky's dad said he'd drive me home. We started out at Urban Outfitters. Mignon bought a t-shirt, but she asked me first what I thought. Frankly, I would've liked anything she wanted to buy. Occasionally Mignon and I would bump together and I could feel her leaning into me like she wanted to be close. Of course, just when I started thinking that maybe I should take her hand or brush her hair back or something, Jeannie would jump in, holding up some piece of junk she wanted Mignon's opinion on.

When David finally showed up, we walked over to the food court. We were all pretty hungry. We ate fast. I had a burger. Mignon had a salad and an apple. She is very health conscious and is considering becoming a full-time vegetarian. Somebody suggested we go to the movies. That got voted down, so we went to the Apple store and messed around. David said he was bored and wanted to go to the game store. The girls wanted to shop. I just wanted to be with Mignon, but standing around the rest of the day while she shopped would have been a big drag. So me and Micky left. But at least, for a few hours, my mind was off the vastness of space and my tiny place in the universe.

▪

One day the next week in science class, Mr. Henkel started talking about geology. It wasn't in our curriculum that term, but somebody had asked him about the rock he kept on his desk. Mr. Henkel is a very calm teacher. He's been at the school for at least 20 years. His beard is half-grey, like his hair, and he has big, friendly eyes, like a spaniel. Sometimes if somebody wasn't paying attention those big eyes would narrow down to slits and you'd know trouble was coming. That morning he was in a good mood, so he held up the rock and let his lesson plan slide.

"This rock—well, I got it on a trip that I took out west, to Arizona to be exact." The rock looked heavy. He kept a tight grip. "This rock actually started out as wood," he told us.

"Wow!" said Sally Kirkland.

"Yes. It's petrified wood. 'Petrified' is a word from the Greek 'petros,' which means 'stone.' What is it, Peter?"

Peter Tillery was waving his hand. He's the neatest

boy in school. His clothes are always pressed and clean, his shoes are always shined, and his hair is always perfectly combed to the side.

"Mr. Henkel, 'Peter' means 'stone,' too. That's why, in the Bible, Christ says 'on this rock I will build my church'—the rock being Saint Peter."

"That's right. And I guess you know that because your name is Peter?"

"Yes, sir." Peter seemed to glow as he looked around at us.

"Anyway, this rock—this piece of petrified wood—is very old. How old do you think it is? Anybody care to guess?"

I volunteered. "Twenty thousand years old." I knew that was wrong, but just wanted to get the ball rolling.

"Nope. Much more."

"One hundred thousand," Sally Kirkland chirped.

"Not close." Mr. Henkel paused for the drama. "It's hard to date it exactly, but this piece of petrified wood could be around 50 million years old."

A gasp from the classroom. Fifty million earth years. Shorter than light years, but a very long time, I thought.

"After class you can come up and look at it if you like. You can still see the tree rings in the stone."

Peter was waving his hand again.

"Yes, Peter."

"My Dad and our preacher say the earth is only about 8,000 years old. Says so in the Bible."

Mr. Henkel paused. He put the petrified wood down on his desk. "Well, Peter, that's what some people believe and that's their right, but scientists believe that the earth is much older than that and the evidence is in the elements that make up our planet."

"How old do they say the Earth is?" I asked.

"Well, present estimates are around 4.5 billion years."

"When in doubt, I go with the Bible," Peter shouted. "Yes, sir, that's what I do and what good people do." His voice was very tense. Before Mr. Henkel could react, the bell rang and people headed out the door. Sally and I went up to the desk to look at the rock. From the back of the room the rock had just looked like a dark, jagged stone but up close it had other colors in it. And you could see the rings.

"Awesome," I said to Mr. Henkel. He wasn't listening. He was looking at Peter, who hadn't moved since the bell. He was just sitting at his desk, like he was in a trance.

"Peter, you want to take a look?" Mr. Henkel asked.

At that, Peter slammed his book shut and dashed out the door without a word.

■

That afternoon we had a big cross-country meet. Teams from Carthage and Madison were there, and also from Dayton Day and Copeland. So five schools were competing. The weather was great, sunny but cool. After a bit of stretching, we all lined up. I love the start of a race. Everybody's jostling around for position, and it's a big group of guys. Maybe 60 or 70 runners. I usually get behind Grady Morris. He's our best runner. He's thirteen, skinny as a rail, and tall. His legs are real long, so he doesn't have to churn like Danny Schenk, who's two or three inches shorter than me and has a little potbelly. But don't sell Danny short. (Pun.) He can run. He makes a funny kind of snorting noise all through the race. He says it helps his breathing, but I think he's just trying to spook other runners around him. They might think he's going to go into a convulsion or that he has some kind of contagious disease. Just when they're concentrating on him, he'll hock up a big wad and spit it off the trail. That usually clears the space around him quick.

When the stampede started that day I was feeling pretty good. Grady got a jump and I was about five yards behind him when we reached the forest. Other guys were wasting energy bolting to the front of the pack, dodging other runners in the process. I just kept a steady pace. I knew that Grady would just hustle along until the mid-point. The runners would have stretched out by then. That's when he'd pick up the pace. And that's where I usually drifted back. It was also the place where I'd hear Danny coming up behind me, snorting and spitting.

This day, though, I tried to keep up with Grady. Well, that's not really right, because I wasn't thinking about keeping up with him at all. I was still thinking about the stars and the universe and all that stuff as I was running. I was thinking how funny it was that we humans lost out in giant space on this little planet were running a race through the woods. Somehow these same thoughts that had scared me weeks before got me to relax. I was running but I wasn't thinking about running. My mind was on everything else. The trees still held some leaves.

A few of the leaves drifted down to the trail. Some fat and curvy clouds to the west were sliding east. Then I saw some glimmer of a planet or star or something near the horizon. Who or what created all that stuff? I know what Mignon would say, and there's no reason to argue with her about it.

So I'm thinking about a creator and I'm running better than I ever have. I didn't know that I was running better at the time, but I felt good at a point in the race when I usually would struggle. My legs didn't seem as tired. The final 200-yard stretch was uphill. You run out of the last of the trees and try to sprint to the finish line. Grady had already finished in first place, followed by two boys from Copeland and one Double-A pal from Dalton. Grady was cheering the team on from the finish line as Randy Carson, a classmate, passed me. I was still ahead of Danny, but I could hear him coming close.

"Go, Taj," he rasped. "You might get third."

Danny and I sprinted up the hill together. He kept encouraging me with his made-up rap: "Gadagga gadagga abababa." Something like that. I can't reproduce the sound he was making. Let's just say I was laughing all the way up the hill. He slowed down some and let me finish third on our team for the first time in my cross-country career. Mignon had kept my time and it was my best, too.

Grady came over. "Good going Tommy." He slapped me on the back.

Best of all, Mignon gave me a hug. Then I flopped on my back and let my whole body get loose. Mignon squatted down next to me. I could smell her perfume. It was like the jasmine bush by our front door. "My hero," she joked.

"Yeah, so I only get a hug?"

"Maybe something more later. When there aren't so many people around."

"Like what?"

She stood up. "It's not going to be what you're thinking."

"What do you think I'm thinking?" I asked.

"Please!" She gave me a hard stare.

"See you later?"

"I've got piano," she said.

"Maybe at the park, before dinner?"

"We'll see."

With that she jogged off. Dad and Mom waited at the top of the hill. Ella was playing with some other kids on a mini sand dune. Dad was smiling and Mom gave me one of her big hugs.

"Well, Tommy, you were right in there. You were. I'm proud of you." Dad high-fived me.

"Tired?" Mom asked.

"Not really. I hardly got a sweat."

Dad had driven the BMW and I sat in the back next to Ella, who was drinking a Gatorade. Mom fiddled with the radio, trying to find some music she liked. Dad was making his own music with the gears as he shifted out on the bypass. Ella looked up from her DS and gave me a poke. I gave her one back. She just laughed.

When I got to the park later, I wasn't worried about the universe. I was worried that Mignon wouldn't show up. And then I was worried that I was worried. I mean, it told me that I really liked her in a way more than I could figure out. And it was cold. They said arctic air was coming tonight. The sun was about to set and a breeze was kicking up. A couple of mothers and their little kids were playing down by the jungle gym. One kid was complaining that it was too cold. I was about to leave when Mignon came speeding down the road. She hit both brakes and the bike slid across the dirt.

"Great slide."

"Thanks."

"I was about to leave."

"Sorry. I had to talk to my dad about something. He likes to talk and once he gets going it's hard to stop him." She dropped her bike next to mine.

"Something bad?"

She just shrugged. "Damn, it's cold."

"Winter's finally getting here." I said the obvious, as usual.

"I don't like the cold, really." She was shivering inside her big jacket.

"Me, neither."

"Unless it snows. Then it's fun."

"We had a good snow last year." I said.

"Yeah. We got a sled and spent all day going down Churchill. That was great."

We were walking while we talked. We reached the creek and without thinking we went down to the rocks. I was feeling great from the race but I was a nervous wreck. I wanted to do the impossible. I took a deep breath. My confidence was teetering.

"You want to go to the movies with me next Saturday?" My voice sounded strange, more like a squawk. Mignon stopped. My stomach was turning. Had I gone crazy? There was a long silence as the question sunk in.

"Like a date?" she asked. I felt my face getting hot.

"I don't know if that's what you call it. Just go to the movies. Hang out."

She stared at me, like she was waiting for the joke. My stomach jittered.

"Well, next Saturday I have a party and a sleepover at Elaine Frish's. Jeannie is going, too, and Lisa."

"So that's a 'no'?"

"I guess so. Sorry."

I was sinking. I turned over a rock with my boot. A crayfish had been hiding there. I grabbed him and held it up to her face. Mignon edged back. "That doesn't scare me. In Louisiana we used to eat those things in big stews." I dropped him back in the water.

"What do you want for Christmas?" she asked me out of the blue.

"I'd like a new phone. Something I could play games on."

"I love my phone," she said. "Listen." She played something by Katy Perry. I couldn't really listen because I was still feeling like crap. I'd finally had the guts to ask her on a real date and she'd said "no." I felt like such a loser. I wanted to join that crayfish under the rock. Mignon turned off the music. I needed to pee.

"What's wrong with you?" she asked.

"I need to pee." It's funny how when you get tense or nervous you suddenly have to pee.

"Go behind a tree."

I went behind the giant pine tree. Nobody could see me from the road. My dick felt the cold and when my pee hit the rocks and roots it seemed to smoke up.

"I can see your pee," Mignon shouted to me.

"So?" I trotted back.

"I wish I could pee like a boy," she said, thinking out loud.

Sometimes you feel colder than it actually is.

"I got to go," I muttered.

"Are you mad?" she asked.

"About what?"

"About Saturday."

"No. I'm not mad."

She stared at me again. "You're upset. I can tell. I would go if Mom would let me and I think she'd be okay with it. I would go. It's just that I have this thing planned. It's Elaine's birthday."

"How old is she?

"Thirteen. She looks fifteen."

I was still feeling kind of embarrassed or something, because I didn't want to talk about it anymore. It was full on twilight now. Almost dark but the sky was rose and blue where the sun was setting. I started home. Mignon grabbed my sleeve and pulled me back. "Hey!" she said. "Don't leave like that. Don't be a baby."

"I gotta go," I said, shaking off her grip.

"I like you. You know it."

I felt my face heat up again. I hoped it wasn't red. "Really?" I wasn't convinced.

"I promised you something after the race, and I keep my promises."

Then she leaned against me, turned her head so our noses wouldn't bump and kissed me on the lips and held the kiss there as her arms came around me. For a second I didn't know what to do, but as she pulled away, I hugged her back for an instant. She gave me a look like she was waiting for me to say something. But I didn't. It was my first real genuine kiss.

"See you later," she said. She jogged back to her bike and took off, pedaling like she was being chased. She did look back once. And she probably saw me standing there waiting to calm down. (Boner alert.) I didn't wave or anything. But she twanged the bell on her bike and I took that as a signal that things were okay.

CHAPTER FIVE

WHAT HAPPENED IN the park in that twilight is what you call an incident. This incident caused me to think about what's most important on this planet, and it requires me to make a short detour and explain something I've been thinking about. From my own twelve-year-old observation, the two most important forces on the planet are gravity and sex. Gravity has always mystified me and I don't think I'm alone. Nobody seems to be able to explain it totally but they keep trying. Even Mr. Henkel, when he has tried, seems to get tied up in knots and ends up at the same place he started. It's funny. I remember talking about it with Micky and Kareem and Mignon one day by the basketball court.

"Right now, we're just standing on an angle." I had their attention.

"Or sitting," Mignon said.

"Or sitting kind of sideways, but you don't know it."

"And I'm jumping sideways?" Kareem asked.

"Yep. Give me the ball." Kareem handed me the ball.

"Say this is Earth and right here by the valve thing is our city. It's above the equator, which is the Spaulding writing. If we're standing right there it's a real angle."

"You're right," Kareem said, taking his ball back and staring at it as if it was Earth.

"Gravity keeps us from just flying off the planet," I said.

"You'd think we'd get kind of dizzy from it," Mignon said.

"But we don't. We don't even notice it." In the end everybody I ever talked to about gravity realized how important it was to everything.

Now for the sex part. I know I'm just twelve (almost thirteen) and between you and me I'm not totally clear on everything about sex. But I do know that no matter what country or how poor or rich people are, it's a big subject. Maybe it's the most important subject for people. Adults tell us what they feel is important: hard work, honesty, love. They want us to be good citizens and help our neighbors. They want peace in the world, too, I guess. But it's pretty clear that what they're really interested in is sex. Almost every ad you see in a magazine or on TV has sex in it. The big ones are for perfume and makeup stuff. Pretty girls with big boobs looking at you from the page or the screen like you were a big plate of Mom's lasagna. They are selling everything from cars to chicken wings. There are ads for vacations with girls in bikinis splashing in the surf inviting you in for a swim. "What happens in Vegas stays in Vegas." How about the beer ads with the guys hustling the girls who all look hot and everybody is having a great time?

But it's not just girls. There are male models with perfect abs strutting around selling god knows what but it's all about sex, I'm sure about that. (Just a word. I don't have perfect abs and I don't think I'll ever have them. My dad, who is pretty darn strong, doesn't have them so it's probably not in our DNA.)

How about the TV shows? Sex is the main subject of a lot of shows, if it isn't somebody getting shot or an autopsy. And don't mention the porno stuff that's all over the Internet. I don't look for it, but some guys do. On TV you see those Cialis and Viagra ads for the older dudes. Seems like they need help getting a boner and those pills are the cure. They have a man and woman looking at each other in the hot tub or dancing in the living room giving each other the sly look. Of course they warn you that you could get dizzy or throw up or go blind or deaf and have a boner that lasts for days. Think of that. Blind and maybe deaf and you can't get rid of it, sticking out like a flagpole for a week.

Speaking of boners, this reminds me of the first time I had a boner that I associated with a girl. A couple of years ago (I think I was in double digits, like ten) we were having a class picnic at Pullen Park. It was springtime and the flowers were blooming. Mrs. Roberts, Jane Roberts's mother, was taking a bunch of us to the park in her Audi convertible. That is a neat ride, I think.

Jane's in the front seat with her mother, and David and I are in the back when we go to pick up Ava Chamblee.

Ava was at dance class. We stopped at the dance studio and out came Ava. She was wearing her leotard and tights and that was it except for her bag, which she tossed in the trunk. Ava was about six months older than me and she had a figure starting. Blonde, curly hair and blue eyes. Boob buds showing. Anyway, she crawled into the back-seat between David and me, all the while ignoring us and talking to Jane. She had a skirt in her hands, which she squirmed into while we were riding along. I have to say I thought she was very pretty but stuck up. Anyway, she kept rubbing against me, because it was tight in the back-seat. Then all of sudden, boing! Jimmy was at attention. I thought it was going to burst my shorts, and I wiggled a bit to try and put the thing to one side.

"What's wrong with you? You got an itch or something?" Ava asked.

When the car pulled up in the parking lot, Jane and her mother jumped out. David was next, but he knew something was up. Ava gave me a cold look and dashed towards the picnic grounds. I just sat there. I didn't know what to do. I was paralyzed. I didn't want to get up with my pecker pointing north so that everybody could see it. But I couldn't sit in the car all day. David figured it out in a second.

"Taj, let's go. Everybody's here." He said it loud enough so that Mrs. Roberts turned around.

"What's the matter, Tommy?" Mrs. Roberts asked me.

"Nothing. Could I just sit here for a minute?"

"Okay," she said with a scrunched up face.

This was before I had a phone. Now I could fake a

phone call from home and stall. But on this day I was about to panic. "I just love this car. I just want to sit in it for a minute. Look it over. Is that okay? I won't mess with anything."

"All right, but I'm leaving in about five or ten minutes." She seemed annoyed.

"That's fine."

When he stopped laughing, David leaned over the door. "Fine? You'll never get rid of that in five minutes," he said.

"Shut up, asshole. You're no help."

"What do you want me to do?" David asked. He seemed a little flustered too.

"I don't know. I'm trapped."

"I heard that cold works. I could get a cold Sprite or something and you could dunk it. That would do it."

"Who'd you hear that from?" I asked.

"Sam, my brother. He's fifteen!"

He said fifteen like it was a magic number.

"Okay. Go." I was desperate.

David sped off to get the Sprite. I sat there thinking, how was I going to dunk my Jimmy in the Sprite without anybody noticing? Other cars were pulling into the parking lot. I started thinking about the baseball game tomorrow and what was going to be for dinner on Sunday. I even thought about Jesus at the Last Supper, like the painting. Luckily, by the time David came back with a cup of Sprite, it was gone. I let out a sigh and jumped out of the car. I didn't want to waste anything so I took a swig of the Sprite. It wasn't very cold.

So there it is. Just think about it. The two most powerful forces on the planet: gravity and sex, and we don't really know much about either one.

Excuse me for meandering. "Meander" is one of my new words and I've been using it lately. When I looked up the definition on the Internet, I learned Meander was the name of a river in ancient Greece that went back and forth and swirled around before it got to where it wanted to go. That's a pretty accurate description of how my mind works and probably how I write. I like finding new words. The problem is knowing where and when to use them.

■

Three houses down from my house, on the corner of Mordecai, lives Dr. Bugg. He isn't a medical doctor. He was a professor at the university, but now he's retired. Dr. Bugg is an expert on (you guessed it) bugs. He's an entomologist. He told me that's the correct name for someone who studies insects. He's a nice man with a shaggy mustache and a bald head with a curly fringe. Some years ago, after he was fully retired from teaching, he converted his garage into a full-scale workshop. He has saws and lathes and all kinds of equipment in there and you can usually find him working on something every day. It might be furniture or a bird house or some kind of art thing. He even designed his gutter spouts out of copper to look like the mouths of frogs, which, of course, eat insects.

When I was younger, I'd take my scooter or bike and ride down to his house just to watch him work. I'd sit by him for an hour and just watch him do something. He never asked me to leave. Occasionally we'd talk about his favorite subject. It started with my interest in ants.

"I see different types—big red ones and little black ones," I said.

"I suspect the little black ones are *Monomorium minimum*. They're pretty common around here. And the red ones could be Argentines, Linepithema humile. They're pretty invasive. But I'd have to see them. There's more than 20,000 species of ants."

"Wow."

He turned off his saw and looked at the cut.

"Can I ask you a question, Dr. Bugg?"

"Sure thing, Thomas."

"Did your name make you interested in bugs when you were my age?"

He laughed a big strong laugh. And then he nodded.

"You know, you have a point. My friends were always kidding me about my name, and they made all kinds of insect jokes. So I think, in self-defense, maybe, I got interested in bugs. I paid attention to them and when I learned about them, I admired them, as well. There were so many types with so many good or interesting qualities. So when I got kidded, in self defense I brought up some insect facts to impress my friends."

"Like what?" I asked.

"Well, since you brought them up, an ant can lift twenty times its own weight. If you had the strength of an ant, you could go out in the driveway and pick up my Subaru and hold it over your head."

I laughed at that idea then and I still think about it now. The Subaru's still in Dr. Bugg's driveway.

■

One afternoon, several weeks after the planetarium visit, I was pedaling through the neighborhood. I saw Dr. Bugg working in his garage. I dropped my bike in his yard and walked over to him. "What are you making?" I asked.

"Some birdhouses, for Christmas presents."

"We've still got the one you gave us."

"Good. Good. How's your mom and dad?"

"Fine." I was itching to get my question in. "Can I ask you something?"

"Of course." He stopped, folded his arms, and sat down on his stool.

"Well, I went with my class to the planetarium over in Chapel Hill the other day and we saw a show about the universe and all different galaxies and stars and black holes and whatever. I've been trying to get my mind around it ever since."

"Good luck. Just thinking about that stuff can wear you out."

"You can say that again." I paused, trying to get my question right. "Do you think there's other life out there somewhere, so that we're not the only planet with life on it?"

He stretched his arms out before he answered, trying to relax, I guess. "Thomas, this is almost a religious question. But, if I were a gambling man, and I've gambled a little in my life, I'd say the chances are very good that

there are other forms of life on other planets somewhere out in space. It just seems sensible to me. Now it
might not be butterflies and puppy dogs. It might just
be simpler life forms, like algae, or lichen, or even something as complex as—shall I say—insects. But I think it's
really possible. I feel like there's a force for life in the
universe, just like on Earth."

"I sure hope so."

"Why's that?"

"It'd be kind of lonely otherwise, don't you think?"

Dr. Bugg laughed his same old big laugh. "Yep. Very
lonely."

"Thanks," I said and sprinted to my bike. "I got to get
home."

"Come back any time, Thomas. Say hello to your
folks."

"Yes, sir." I don't know why talking to him made me
feel a little better, but it did.

CHAPTER SIX

THE CROSS COUNTRY season was ending. We went to our last meet and had our group party at Andy's Pizza. I got the little trophy for most improved. I was happy about that. I've never gotten many trophies, except for those soccer ones that they give to everybody. They're a joke. You want a trophy to mean something.

My concerns about the universe and all that space stuff kept coming up now and then. When I went to the library with Mom and Ella, I'd somehow always drift over to the Science section and look for books on the stars. Some were just full of pictures. They even had photos of things called nebulae. There was one they call the Pillars of Creation, with these big tall clouds of stuff. It was very beautiful. From my Googling it seems that nebulae are where new stars are born. Then there are supernovas where stars die. They just kind of explode.

It's too much to try and understand in one minute. You keep asking yourself, "Where are we?" "What are we doing here?" "Are we just an accident?" That would be sad, wouldn't it? Just an accident. When I say something like that to Mignon, she just laughs and says something like, God is smarter than you or me or Micky or Mr. Henkel. "You should go to church more," she'd say.

We do go to church. Mom takes Ella and me to Aycock Methodist Church almost every Sunday. I sometimes go to Sunday school and we do some Bible work, which is interesting. I like the old stories. Like about Noah and Jonah and Samson. You know they're exaggerated but whoever thought them up had a great imagination. I can hear Ella down the hall cackling. She thinks the stories are funny. One time our Bible study was reading some Old Testament passages in Ecclesiastes. Everybody has heard that one section: "To everything there is a season, and time to every purpose under heaven. . . ." It goes on and on and it can be kind of depressing, or interesting, depending on your mood.

At the end of the chapter though, after the familiar part, I remember this verse, and I'm gonna write it down just the way it is in my Bible. "He hath made everything beautiful in his time, also he hath set the world in their heart, so that no man can find out the work that God maketh from the beginning to the end."

Trying to understand this, I asked Mr. Potter, the Sunday school teacher, about it and he wasn't very clear, except that the "He" was God. Mr. Potter, who sells insurance, is a tall thin man with a big sharp nose. He rubs that beak when he's thinking. My question made him rub his nose a lot.

"I'm gonna check the concordance about that and

get back to you. Good question, Tommy."

I agree that the world has a lot of beauty in it, like those nebulae and even something as ordinary as a little dandelion. But what I think the verse is saying is that you cannot know what God knows. You can't figure out what I'm trying to figure out. You'll just be frustrated. You just have to accept that you don't know what's really going on. That's what Mignon's saying to me, I think. Yet we have scientists constantly working on finding out about everything from the smallest thing to the largest thing. They want to know why things happen. They aren't satisfied with being in the dark. Honestly, I just think some people are more curious than others. You can count me in the curious group. And if you're in that group, you can't stop asking questions or looking for new ways to do things. That's pretty obvious.

■

Now comes the hard part of my story. The downer part. It started with a phone call.

My uncle, Aaron, was older than my dad. He'd gone to college and after teaching history at a high school over in Greensboro for three years, he went to work for a bank. He did a good job, I guess, because he kept getting promoted and became a vice-president in the main building with a big office and a secretary, etcetera. So he had a job where you had to wear a coat and tie. He always tried to look sharp. But on the weekends he dropped that and put on his leathers. He had a big Harley that he liked to ride when the weather was good. Sometimes Aunt Mary

Rose would ride with him. They'd take trips to the mountains up around Boone or Asheville. They always came through town when they were headed for the beach. He always had a good joke or two to tell you and unlike a lot of older people, he didn't lay on the advice.

Well, three weeks before Christmas break, he was riding that big Harley out in the country. It was twilight and he was heading home when a kid in a pickup truck ran a stop sign and clipped him. He and the bike went sailing. He ended up in a ditch a ways down the road. The kid in the pickup had a bloody nose but Uncle Aaron was dead.

Aunt Mary Rose called Dad that night and after he hung the phone up, he just stood there letting the news sink in. Finally he turned around. Mom already knew something was really wrong.

"Aaron is dead," Dad said. He stopped for a moment and shook his head real slow. "He got killed on his Harley, out near Biscoe. I have to go up there. I can't believe it... just like that."

"My, lord. I'm sorry, Rick. That's awful. Can I do something for Mary Rose?"

"Maybe later. She sounded, well, kind of in shock, like you'd expect. I'll call you when I get there."

"Okay. Be safe," Mom said. I think she wanted to say more but couldn't find the words.

Dad grabbed his jacket and headed out the door. He took the pickup.

Ella walked in with her monster doll in her hand. "What's the matter?"

Mom just looked at her for a moment. "Dad had to go do something. You have to get ready for dinner."

"What are we having?"

"Pasta and some broccoli."

"Ugh."

"Well, you're gonna try it." Mom was serious.

Ella scampered back to her room.

"Tommy, have you done your homework?"

I was standing in the middle of the kitchen, thinking about the news I'd just heard.

"Most of it."

"Then wash up and set the table."

"Just for us three, right?"

She nodded and I went to the sink and got the soap. The water was boiling on the stove and Mom was dumping in the pasta. I think she was crying, but she wiped her eyes with her apron and went on about her business. I set the table and waited until Mom asked me to go get Ella. Ella didn't want to leave her room with broccoli on the horizon.

"I ain't eating it," Ella said.

"Just try it."

"I've tried it and it's awful."

"Put a bunch of salt on it. Mix it up with the spaghetti," I suggested.

"I could use ketchup," she said, thinking out loud.

"That's a great idea." I said but it sounded gross.

"I'm sick," she blurted out with a cough.

"No, you're not. Don't make me go through this. I'll play Mario with you after I do my homework."

"This is not a trick?" Ella asked.

"Nope."

"Okay."

We marched on down. Ella went straight for the ketchup.

That night after Dad had called and told Mom what was up, I crawled into bed, but I couldn't sleep right away. The house seemed really quiet that night. Ella walked in. She stood by my bed and stared at me.

"What?"

"What's going on?"

I didn't want to say anything, but I knew she'd just keep standing there all night if necessary.

"Uncle Aaron, he got killed. Riding his motorcycle."

"Killed?"

"Yep."

"Dead?"

"Yeah."

"That's terrible," she said. "That's where Dad was going?"

"Yep."

She stood there for a long time and then she started to cry. Not loud, but the new tears were running slowly down her cheek. "I love Uncle Aaron," she said.

"Me, too."

"It makes me mad." Her face squinched up like she was aching.

"He loved that Harley," I said.

She nodded. "Can I sleep in here with you?"

Now, normally I would've said, "No, no, no," but on this night, with this sad, bad news, I didn't. She crawled in beside me and then Jake trotted up. His tail wasn't wagging as usual. He could tell something bad had happened. He waited for a second, and then jumped in the bed, too. He curled right by my feet and stayed there all night.

▪

The funeral was held at the Antioch Baptist Church a few days later in the afternoon. The sky was bright blue. A few fluffy clouds were up there and they seemed out of place. The church building was new and important looking. A white church with a high steeple. It was prettier and larger than the Methodist church we went to. Grandmother and Grandfather Johnson flew up from Florida. They looked much older than when I last saw them. Granddad was using a cane. Grandma seemed shaky sitting in the pew. The family all sat together in the front of the church. The casket was on a table right in front of the altar. Big vases of flowers were on both sides of the casket with some other flower baskets all around the bottom of the table. The smell of the flowers was stronger than Mom's perfume. I didn't like it. It said something sad to me.

Aunt Mary Rose sat in front of us sniffling into a handkerchief. Aaron Junior was next to her. He's sixteen. His brother, Billy, sat next to him. Billy's fourteen and he has an affliction called cerebral palsy, which makes him bent over and herky-jerky when he walks. But when I've been around him he's been very cheerful, especially considering his condition. I don't think I could be that pleasant, feeling like that, but you never know. My dad said that you can't worry about things that you can't change (sounds like Mignon) and that you have to deal with the good and the bad in life. And he's right. But still, you don't know how you'll deal with something until you have to.

A pretty woman who turned out to be Aunt Mary Rose's cousin sang a hymn, and then the preacher got up and introduced Uncle Aaron's boss from the bank. He was a small man with a large head but he spoke very well, like he'd had some speaking classes in college. Basically he wanted to say good things about Uncle Aaron.

"He was an excellent coworker—not an employee, because we were like family. But as good as he was to work with, he was even better as a friend. He will be sorely missed." That was the gist of what he was saying, and I thought it was nice to be remembered that way. Then Dad got up. He was clutching a piece of paper on which he had written what he wanted to say about his brother. You could tell he was nervous, but he stood up there and looked out over the congregation.

"My brother was the best brother anybody could ever have. He kept me out of trouble more times than I care to remember. When I needed a shoulder to lean on, Aaron was always there. Sometimes I didn't have to ask. He just knew me and knew when I needed a good word or a smile or a kick in the butt. I know he loved you, Mary Rose, and you, Aaron Junior and Billy. He never stopped talking about how lucky he was to have this family." At that point, Mary Rose went from crying to weeping, and Dad was choking up himself. Ella wouldn't look up at him. She was holding a hymnal and looking through the pages. "We don't know why he was taken from us so young, so full of life. That's God's mystery. And we just have to accept it. But I'm having a hard time with it and I'll miss him more than I want to admit. God bless you, Aaron. Rest in peace."

With that, Dad walked down the steps and back to the pew and sat down next to Mom. The preacher, a man with a round face and round glasses, got up and gave a short talk about the resurrection and the promise of Christ. He talked about "Aaron's faith" and his love of Jesus and family and Greensboro. And Harley Davidson. After that little sermon, the congregation sang "Amazing Grace," several verses, and that was that for the church service. Then we piled into a couple of limos for the trip to the cemetery.

The cemetery was big and hilly—a good place to sled after a snow if it wasn't for all the tombstones and markers. We rode slowly to the top of one hill. The grave had already been dug. A couple of amigos were standing a ways away with their equipment, watching and waiting. I guessed they would fill in the grave after we had all left. The undertakers had brought most of the flowers from the church and put them under the tent that covered the grave area. The casket was brought from the Cadillac hearse and carried to a contraption over the grave. You could see the red clay clumped around the edge of the dark cloth they had laid down. The preacher said a few more words and then a little prayer. What I remember about that, because I had heard it before on a TV show, was "Ashes to ashes, dust to dust." I wondered about the ashes part.

After that, a man playing a bagpipe seemed to appear from nowhere. The piper stood by himself between the amigos and the tent and he played another version of "Amazing Grace." A cold wind was whipping up now, even though the sun was out. The piper's kilt was flapping in the wind. For whatever reason, that bagpipe music made everybody a little sadder than they were before, or maybe it was watching the casket get lowered slowly into the hole while the music played. When the piper stopped, there was another prayer for all of us sinners and the ceremony broke up. Aunt Mary Rose tossed a bunch of little flowers that she had been holding into the grave. After that everybody went and lined up to pay their respects to Aunt Mary Rose and Aaron Junior and my Dad. Grandma and Granddad kept their seats.

Billy stood there for a minute or two and then he ambled off into the old part of the cemetery. It wasn't easy for him to shake hands. I thought I should go over and tell him I was sorry and whatever. The part of the cemetery where Uncle Aaron was being buried was new. They had scraped off all the trees and planted grass. There was a little building where I think they put some of the dead people who didn't want to be in the ground. But a little ways down the hill was the oldest part of the cemetery. Big trees were scattered around that part with big monuments for the departed. Billy shuffled around looking at the tombstones.

"Eighteen eighty three," he said.

I looked at the old tombstone. Underneath the date they had carved, "Abide with me". "Sorry about your Dad, Billy."

"Thanks."

"You been okay?"

"Yeah. Mom's taking it pretty hard."

"Yeah. I'm sure."

"Look at this. Eighteen fourteen. Wow."

It was a grave for a little child, born in 1810. "At home with Jesus" was carved into the tombstone.

"This is an old cemetery." I sometimes say the obvious.

"People die all the time. That's the way it is." Billy was fighting a cold. He pulled a rumpled handkerchief from his coat pocket and blew his nose.

"You still helping out with the baseball team?" I asked.

He rocked a little. "Yeah. They made me honorary manager. Such bullshit."

"Kind of an honor."

"You know it's bullshit."

He stopped and I was worried he was going to fall over. His body was shaking. I went over just to give him some support and I saw the tears in his eyes.

"It's bullshit." This time he almost yelled it.

I put an arm around his shoulders. I don't know exactly why.

"I'm gonna miss my daddy," he said.

"Sure enough," I said. "He really loved you. And that's not bullshit."

He took a couple of deep breaths, pulling himself together.

"Billy!" Aunt Mary Rose was calling him.

The crowd was breaking up and heading back to their cars.

"We're coming," I shouted back.

Me and Billy walked slowly back up that hill. A couple of times he stumbled and I could see the brace on his left leg when his pants lifted. "Cold, ain't it?" It wasn't really a question.

He nodded. "I hate the winter," Billy said.

Aunt Mary Rose moved towards us, and before he headed for his limo Billy turned to me. "Come up some time. We're cousins, you know."

"I'm sure we will."

Aunt Mary Rose gave me a pat and I gave a nod to Aaron Junior. He shrugged back. I caught up with Mom and Dad and Ella and we headed for our car.

"How's Billy?" Mom asked.

"Okay," I lied. What was the use of saying more?

■

We went over to Uncle Aaron's house. It's a really nice house—brick, with a fancy door and antique furniture around. People were congregating in the kitchen and dining room. The neighbors had brought cakes and pies and some casseroles. The food was set out on the dining room table along with an urn of coffee and pitchers of iced tea and water. A pretty girl named Mabel helped serve. She had short brown hair and big green eyes.

Everything about her seemed soft and round. She could have been fifteen.

"You're Tommy," she said, handing me a piece of Bundt cake and a cup of water.

"Yep."

"Nice to meet you. I think we're cousins," she said with a big smile.

"For real?"

"I'm Mabel. I'm Aunt Mary Rose's niece."

"Do you live around here?"

"No. I live in Charlotte."

"Is it nice?" I asked.

"It's okay. We might move to Atlanta."

"I've never been there."

"Me neither. I'd rather stay in Charlotte."

A woman came up and gave both of us a smile. "Honey, could I have a piece of that lovely cake?"

"Yes, ma'am."

The serving table was getting crowded, so I decided to head back to where Ella was sitting in the living room. "Thanks for the cake," I said.

"You're welcome," Mabel said, and waved. She seemed like a nice cousin.

The eating and talking went on for quite a while. Aunt Mary Rose seemed to have stopped crying and was chatting with everybody she could and thanking them for coming by. It was interesting to me that the day ended up like this. Some people were laughing. Some people were bumping into old friends they hadn't seen for a while. Aaron Junior was chatting up Mabel now and she was smiling at whatever he was saying. And here I was, looking at her nice big breasts in the middle of this sad event—a wake somebody called it. Was that bad? I didn't see Billy anywhere. I suspect all the noise didn't agree with him and so he went to his room to be quiet and think.

Dad and Mom talked to Aunt Mary Rose for a long while, then it was time to head home. Ella had fallen asleep on the couch in the living room and Dad carried her to the car. Mabel and her mom and dad had left earlier. Some neighbors were cleaning up, washing dishes and sweeping the kitchen floor as we headed into the twilight. Driving back was different. The trip seemed a lot longer than it had in the morning. Nobody said much of anything. Mom didn't turn on the radio. Ella was still sleeping. I stared out the window into the lights we were passing. There were billboards for just about everything. Food. Insurance. Cars. The big outlet mall. But I started thinking about Aunt Mary Rose and Aaron Junior and Billy in that big house when all the people had gone home and there was no Uncle Aaron laughing in front of the TV. All his clothes still in the closet and the dresser. Papers still on his desk where he left them. Dirty socks in the hamper. Bottle of Budweiser in the fridge. He was gone and I thought, how would I feel if one day Dad was gone like that? His tools in the garage. His gloves. His Redskins cap.

"I'll go up and check on her next week," Mom said.

"That'll be good." Dad didn't look away from the road.

And that was all that was said until we pulled into our driveway at 10 o'clock.

CHAPTER SEVEN

THE WEATHER GOT even colder before Christmas break. The water in our old birdbath froze solid. We had a few flurries of snow but nothing stuck. The sky was grey and the days were really short. The sun would start going down around five but the sunsets were great, because the sky wasn't blocked by the tree leaves. The sky could be pink and sometimes orange mixed with grey. It could even be black on some days as dark storm clouds sped across.

Mignon and I met down at the park after school. It was really cold, so we walked over to the picnic shed where the wind wasn't so strong. I found a pack of matches in my pocket and we made a small fire in the barbecue grill with some old branches and newspaper from the trash. That took some of the edge off the cold. I told her about the funeral.

She rubbed her hands over the fire. "My grandma died two years ago. She had a bad heart. It was sad."

"Yeah."

"Did you like your uncle?" Mignon asked.

"Yeah, a lot."

"I like my Uncle Trent, too, and Uncle George." She seemed to be remembering them when she spoke.

"Some people don't get along with their families," I said.

She stopped to think a little.

"You know, in New Orleans, when somebody dies, they have a parade, with march music. It's kind of sad and happy at the same time. Because death is just the door. That's the idea. So saying goodbye is kind of a party or something."

"If you're a Christian that's not a bad way to look at it," I said.

"I wonder what other religions think about dying?" Mignon asked.

"I don't know. I did talk to Micky once. He's a Buddhist, or his parents are."

"Yeah, what do they think?" She was in an asking mood.

"From what I can tell, they kind of worship their ancestors, but I think he said some folks might believe in reincarnation—that we come back again as something else."

"Like what?"

"I don't know. Like a person or an animal." That's about as much as I knew.

"I'd like to be a bird. Maybe a parrot," she said with a smile.

"Yeah. Parrots are beautiful and they live a long time.

Me, I'd like to be a big old tortoise. They live a long, long time."

"But you got to carry that shell," she protested.

"So?"

Mignon was staring at the flames. "Some people have no religion. Atheists, they just believe we're gone, like that," she said, snapping her fingers.

There are times when you start thinking and your brain seems to get tied in knots. You just have to stop and take a break. That's where I was. There were other times, looking at Mignon, that I just wanted to give her a hug or even just study her face. This was one of those times. Her face was glowing in the firelight.

"What's wrong?" she asked me.

"Nothing. I just like looking at you."

"You're crazy," she said.

"You think so?"

"I do. But kinda cute."

I was going to thank her for the compliment when Mr. Parker came marching by the park. He was carrying a little flashlight while he walked his dog, Mitzi. She was a mean little animal, always snapping and snarling.

"You kids, what you doing over there?" he yelled.

"Nothing, sir. It's Tommy Johnson and Mignon Eubanks," I answered.

"Put out that fire before you cause a disaster."

"Yes, sir."

He waited, beaming his flashlight at us while I got some dirt to put on the flames. Mitzi was barking and growling. The smoke billowed up. I got more dirt until I was sure the fire was all out.

"Get on home!" Mr. Parker shouted as he turned the corner.

"*Tais-toi!*" Mignon shouted back. I was surprised that she reacted at all. "That's 'shut up' in French," she whispered to me.

"I wish I could cuss and yap in another language."

"Don't you take Spanish?"

"Yeah, but the words I need aren't in the vocab book." It was really dark now without the fire. "I guess we should head back," I said.

"Yeah. I just hate to give in to that old busybody," she muttered.

"I'm giving in to the cold."

We left the picnic shed and stopped under the street light.

"I wish it was Christmas already," I said.

"It's soon. I'm hoping for an iPad. My grades are pretty good this semester." She was shivering now.

"How do you say goodbye in French?"

"*Au revoir.*"

"Well, *au revoir*," I said, as best as I could.

We both started trotting home, burying our hands in our pockets, because of the cold. When she had disappeared, I stopped for a moment and looked up at the sky for the first time in days. The Big Dipper was overhead and hundreds of other twinkling stars in constellations I didn't know. There was only a little cold sliver of a moon. The sky was a question without an answer.

▪

One thing I started doing after the funeral was reading the obituaries in the paper. I never even looked at those pages before, but all of sudden they became interesting. I couldn't help myself. I'd start reading other parts of the paper first but eventually find myself there. Everyday some names and photos appeared. Today's paper has a bunch of obits for people who have passed.

Otis Hyde, pharmacist, member of Kiwanis, Presbyterian, and grandfather to five grandkids. Loved rooting for the Wolfpack. Had a dog named Buster. Died at 71. Send donations to the Jimmy V Foundation.

Dolores Capehart, died at 88, born in Visalia, Georgia. Married to Alan Capehart, who preceded her in death. Baptist. Three children: Amanda, Jake, Reese. Member of the Camellia Club and long supporter of the symphony. Her photo must have been taken when she was about 30. A very pretty face with a curly hairdo.

Darius Fellows, Double A, NAACP, died at 55. Attended North Carolina A &T. Married to Leonora Wicks. One child, Solomon, who's a student at State. Residential contractor for 28 years. Loved traveling. Favorite places were Jamaica and Hawaii. Friendly face. He looks like somebody you'd like to know.

Most everybody in the obituaries is pretty old. But there are some young ones, too.

Tim Critcher. Only 17. "Will be sorely missed." Senior at Garner High School. In the band he played clarinet. Loved to hunt and fish. Got his first big buck last year. Funeral to be held at the Amity Baptist Church on

Saturday. In lieu of flowers send contributions to Mothers Against Drunk Driving.

Savannah Crumpler, 12 years old. Loved to dance and play soccer. Fought the good fight against her disease and cheered up everybody who came in contact with her. Her parents, Dave and Marsha, ask that donations be sent to the Children's Hospital at Duke University. Savannah is not only survived by her parents but also by her younger brother, Zeke.

Every day, more and more little stories are in the obituaries, stories that you could imagine lives from. Some people were big shots with long write-ups. Some were just regular folks, working people with only a paragraph and no photo. You might think reading these obituaries is a little creepy, but I think it makes you realize how life goes by and how you never know when your number is up. People live out their lives and it ends up in a couple of paragraphs in the local paper if you're not famous or a big crook or something. Later, who'll remember them and all the things they cared about?

▪

To say that Uncle Aaron's passing put a damper on Christmas would be an understatement. Usually this was my favorite time of the year. I liked the lights and the tree and all the decorations and traditions. It was also a time for me and Dad to be together more than normal. I would be out of school and he'd have a few days off of work, or at least a shorter schedule. We like football, and we'd sit on the couch and watch all the bowl games we could stomach and all the pro playoff games we were interested in. Dad's a Redskins fan and somewhere along the line I had to pick a team. I didn't want to have the same team as Dad, so when I was 10, I picked the Patriots. Dad was not pleased.

"Why the Patriots?"

"Why not? I like Tom Brady."

"You've never even been close to Massachusetts, or anywhere in New England."

That was true, but it's a place I'd like to go. The American Revolution started up there. Great leaders from Patrick Henry and John Adams and John Kennedy were from there. Harvard's in Boston and MIT, too. And I like Boston cream pie.

"How many times you been to Washington?" I asked Dad.

"It doesn't matter. It was the team we all cheered for because we didn't have a pro team down here then. It was the closest. My dad was a big Redskins fan. Of course, now he's a Miami fan. Turncoat. Why didn't you choose the Panthers? They're local."

"I don't like Charlotte. It's almost South Carolina," I said.

"Well, I'm with you there."

"So I'm sticking with the Patriots."

"You're just a front runner. If they start losing, you'll start looking around."

"If that ever happens."

"Streak can't last forever," Dad suggested.

"You should know. You're a Yankee fan."

"You got me there."

"Let's face it. Tom Brady has the best looking girl-friend or wife or whatever in the league." That was my best argument.

"You got me there, too."

So that's how we ended our discussion. That year, Santa brought me some Patriots gear—a t-shirt and a cap—and I've worn them ever since when I watch the games.

This Christmas, though, Dad didn't watch much football. He stayed in the garage working on the Norton. After Uncle Aaron died on the Harley, I was sure Mom would make him sell the motorcycle, but she didn't. When he wasn't working on the Norton, he kept busy in other ways, as if he didn't want a spare minute to think about things. He cleaned out the gutters. Twice. He replaced some siding on the house. He put some new grout in the bathrooms. He hauled some trash to the dump. I watched a little football, but without Dad there to kid and go back and forth with, it wasn't very interesting. I even tried to help with the Norton, but he seemed like he wanted to work by himself. Ella was one of the Marys in the living nativity scene at the church this year. When we all went to see her one night, one of the shepherd boys passed out and almost killed a sheep. In a minute he was okay and he tried to get back to his place. They got him a chair but that didn't look right. A shepherd with his crook sitting by the manger on a metal folding chair. It's hard to rec-reate stuff.

I went Christmas shopping on the Saturday before Christmas. The mall was packed with what seemed like half the county. Mom dropped me and Kareem off right when the stores opened. Kareem wanted to buy something for his grandmother and his mom. And he had to find something for his girlfriend, Latitia. I wanted to get something for Mom and Dad and Ella and, of course, Mignon. Ella would want something funny. I'd saved money from chores and allowance. I figured I could find something. We'd been there about fifteen minutes when Micky showed up. Micky said he was just hanging out, which was okay. We all went into Victoria's Secret. The shop girls gave us a funny look, especially when Kareem picked up some thong panties and started admiring them.

"She'd look fine in these."

"Her ass is too big for that," Micky chimed in.

"You say what?" Kareem whirled around in mock anger. The shop girls looked ready to call security when we rolled back out the door. We were laughing and joking and getting no shopping done because I think we were too shy or embarrassed to really get down to it.

"I got to get stuff done," Kareem said.

"Yeah. Me too," I said.

"Let's meet back at the food court in an hour."

"Good."

So off we went on separate paths. I found Dad a NC State glass that the lady wrapped up real nice. At Urban Outfitters I bought Ella some cool pink sunglasses. I knew she'd like them. When I turned to go, I bumped right into Mignon.

"Hey," she said.

"Hey." It was a happy surprise.

"What you up to?" she asked.

"Christmas shopping," I said.

"We are, too."

Now I noticed she was standing with the annoying Elaine Frish.

"Hello, Elaine."

"Thanks for noticing," she said. Her new braces made her look dangerous.

"You're hard to avoid," I said.

I think the look on Elaine's face is what's called a sneer.

"C'mon, guys. It's almost Christmas. Did you find anything in here?" Mignon wanted things smooth.

"Just something for Ella."

"Who else do you need to shop for?"

"Mom." I wasn't going to tell her I was looking for her.

"Any ideas?"

"Nope."

Elaine was playing with some necklaces that dangled from a display board. One necklace was leather and had different little charms and junk hanging at the end.

"I like this one," Elaine said.

"Not for me. I like this one, though," Mignon said. She was holding a necklace with a silver, shiny peace symbol on it. She tried it on. You could tell it suited her. "How about perfume?" she said to me.

"Perfume?"

"Yeah, for your Mom. I'm sure she likes perfume."

"I don't know anything about perfume," I said, and that was the honest truth.

"Well, perfume may be too expensive but you can get cologne for less or toilet water."

"Toilet water doesn't sound good."

"Smell this," she said holding up her wrist. "Go ahead."

I leaned over and sniffed the pale skin of her wrist. The smell was fantastic, like jasmine or gardenia, but stronger.

"You like that?"

"Yeah," I said.

"Elaine and I were at Nordstrom, testing and spraying perfume. It's called Madagascar. Like the movie."

"Maybe I'll run over there. I'm meeting up with Kareem and Micky at the food court at 12:30."

"See you there."

I sprinted over to Nordstrom. There was Madagascar, on the corner of the perfume counter. The bottle was oval-shaped with green petals at the top. The perfume was too expensive and the cologne wasn't a lot better for my budget. But the lady at the counter tried to help.

"How about this little sprayer? She can keep it in her purse and whenever she needs a little spritz she can pull it out, just like this."

The thing looked like a lipstick case. It was shiny green and gold.

"I'll take it," I said surprising myself.

"This for your girlfriend?" she asked.

"Naw. For my mom."

"Well, here are some free samples. Maybe she'll like some of these." She gave me a handful of little plastic bottles.

"Thanks. Thanks a lot."

Now my real goal was to race back to Urban Outfitters and buy that necklace that Mignon had liked. I didn't even get the Madagascar wrapped, I was in such a hurry. I found the necklace as soon as I walked in the store. The girl at the cash register had a piercing on her bottom lip and a flower tattoo on her arm. She wasn't in the mood to gift wrap.

By the time I reached the food court, they were all sitting down, eating.

"Where were you?" Mignon asked.

"You get to the perfume counter and you kind of get involved, testing and stuff."

"Some of those girls at the perfume counter are hot," Micky said. I ignored him.

"You got Madagascar?" Mignon asked.

"Yeah."

She smiled. "Good job. Just remember who told you about it."

I could still smell it on her, sweet and flowery.

I got up and went to order my burger, but I didn't have enough money left to get more than a drink. That was okay. There is no better feeling than when you know you have finished Christmas shopping for the main people on your list.

■

Usually on Christmas Day, after the gifts were opened, we'd get together with Uncle Aaron's family, either at our house or his. When it was at our place, we'd invite some other friends over and we would have a big family dinner. Twelve or fourteen people, at least, would be at the table. We'd have ham and turkey and all the extras. Uncle Aaron would usually get in the recliner after dinner and take a little nap. The neighbors would come over for a drink and a joke and we kids would show each other what we got for Christmas. If the weather was good everybody would go out to the deck. If it was snowing, we spread out all over the house, the kids by the television playing Wii games until there was enough snow to sled or have a snowball fight while the grownups drank and gossiped. Mom would make a big bowl of eggnog and I even took a sip last year. It was delicious. I didn't get drunk or anything because I only took a drop.

Let me say this, Christmas is usually a happy time for our family, but not this year. I mean, it was okay. We had the tree and the wreath and the lights in the holly bushes, but no Uncle Aaron and the friends who came by kept it short and sweet. Mom didn't make her eggnog and Dad was drinking a lot of beer. I could tell how much when I carried the bag of cans to the recycling bin. Mom was worried, and once she mentioned to Dad that he might cut down a little. He just gave her a look and a little nod, which wasn't a yes but a maybe. But he kept popping those tabs.

On the brighter side, I got an iPhone for Christmas. It wasn't the latest but it was good enough for me. I couldn't wait to text my friends. Mignon was the first who texted back. "Congrats" and then "Go to FaceTime." It took me a minute or two to figure that out and then we were looking at each other on our phones and she was wearing the necklace I got for her.

"You're a real trickster, aren't you?"

"What do you mean?" I asked like I was innocent.

"That's why you were late getting to the food court. You went back and got this for me."

"So what?"

"Okay. You're so clever."

"Well, thank you," I said.

"Got to go. But thanks again. I really, really like it."

"And thank you for the star map."

"Star Finder," she corrected me. "And you are welcome. See you later. Promise."

The Star Finder that Mignon gave me is this cardboard contraption where you rotate the sky map so that it matches up with the date when you're looking at the night sky. You can locate constellations pretty easy and the brightest stars. Even planets like Venus. It's great. But the best gift I got was the fact that she liked my gift. She hadn't told me whether she had gotten the iPad or any other stuff for Christmas. She just wanted to show me she was wearing that necklace with the peace sign.

CHAPTER EIGHT

THE DAY AFTER Christmas, Mignon went to the mountains with her church group to learn to ski. She sent photos and videos of her progress. The last video she sent was of her coming down the slope pretty fast. She'd figured it out. I knew she would.

Over the break I also texted Kareem and Micky and David and a couple of others. They all seemed pretty content with their Christmases. Santa brought Ella an electric keyboard piano. She started hammering on it as soon as she got it and we all were afraid that she'd never stop. But she finally did when she started reading a book that Aunt Mary Rose had given her. We called that the real Christmas miracle.

Then came another incident. If you check in the dictionary, one of the meanings of "incident" is "an uncommon happening." That's exactly what I mean. We had gotten through Christmas and, like I said, it was kind of a sad/happy Christmas and we were waiting for the New Year. We were still missing Uncle Aaron a lot. No matter how much you liked your presents that was in the back of your mind.

It was a Thursday. Dad had gone to work that day. He'd usually come home around six or six thirty for dinner but this day he didn't show up. Mom called him around seven and he told her something that made her start dinner without him. We had some chicken tenders and sweet potatoes and she broke out the broccoli again.

"Is this some kind of torture?" Ella asked.

"What?"

"You know what."

"You need vegetables," Mom said with a sigh.

"Why not some green beans or carrots, or even zucchini stuff?"

"Broccoli's really good for you."

"I don't believe it. Maybe it gives you vitamins, but it also gives you stress."

Mom shook her head. "Eat one piece and I'll give you a carrot."

Ella popped one in her mouth. Her eyes squeezed shut and she chewed as hard as she could. This distraction allowed me to drop a couple of my pieces to Jake, who seemed to love broccoli.

After dinner, Ella and I played with our Christmas presents for a while. Mom called Dad a couple of times on his cell, but he didn't pick up, so we took our showers and headed to bed. Mom had a worried look but she didn't say anything. She tried to keep things regular.

I dozed off. It must have been around midnight when I heard a big bang outside. I looked out the window and could see Dad's truck, with the lights on, idling in the driveway. He'd stopped at a weird angle and it seemed like he'd hit the big trash can real hard, knocking it over so that half the trash was spilling out. I heard him open the door and stomp into the house. Mom was up, because I could hear her voice, but I couldn't tell what she was saying. I climbed out of bed and snuck down the hall.

"You could have called. I was worried sick," I heard Mom say.

"I told you I was going to have a drink." Dad's voice was slurry.

"You had more than one, Rick."

"So fucking what?" Dad's voice boomed.

"You're driving drunk."

"So I might get killed?" He staggered to a chair and flopped down.

"And you might kill somebody else, too. Some inno-cent person."

Dad sighed and rubbed his head with his hand, like he had a bad headache. I'd seen Dad drink before and get what he called a buzz on, especially when his army buddies came around. He'd get real happy and do some-thing sort of crazy. One time they all played buzzed b'ball in the driveway. One of the guys got a busted nose, but nobody was mad. They were just having fun. But he wasn't happy now. I'd never seen him so messed up—restless in the chair, eyes rolling around, fists clenched up.

"I know you miss Aaron. I know it. I know you're hurting, but this isn't the way to deal with it," Mom said.

"What the hell do you know?"

"I know that Andy called me this afternoon and said he thought you might be drinking at work. He was worried."

With that, Dad shot straight up from his chair.

"That's bullshit!" he shouted. "Goddamn bullshit!"

"Quiet. You're going to wake the kids up."

"Well, in that case, I'm going back out. I need to make some noise."

"No you're not."

Mom's voice was as strong as I'd ever heard it. She grabbed the truck keys from the table.

"Give me those damn keys, Claire!" he roared, lurching towards her.

"No." She took a step back. I think she was scared. I know I was. My stomach was turning. I thought I was going to hurl.

"Give me the goddamn keys!" This time his voice was an angry whisper; his face was twisted. She took another step back and he stumbled towards her. His hand went back as if he was going to swing.

"Dad!" I shouted from the steps. "Stop it!"

He whirled around and saw me on the stairs. I was shaking in my pajamas. I was afraid he was going to hit her or something. Tears were in Mom's eyes but the keys were still clenched in her fist.

"Go back to bed!" Dad yelled up to me.

"No!" I yelled back. I had never spoken to my father like that, ever. I think it surprised him, and he took a deep breath and went to sit down as if he weighed a ton. His arm swung back and knocked a glass off the breakfast table. It shattered into a hundred pieces on the floor.

Shaking his head, he knelt down to pick up the broken glass. Mom looked up at me and shooed me back to bed. "Take Ella with you," she said.

I turned and saw Ella standing behind me, blinking, still half-asleep.

"What's going on?" she asked.

"Nothing," I told her and started to herd her back to bed when I looked back at Mom. She walked over to where Dad was squatting on the floor and touched his shoulder.

"Rick, you okay?" she asked him. He just shook his head.

She sighed and looked back to me again. "Go back to bed, Tommy," she said. "Go!"

I took Ella by the hand. Dad muttered something. Did he say "Sorry"? I hoped so.

After I got Ella tucked away, I sat on my bed and looked at the night sky from my window. I could hear Mom and Dad talking. but I couldn't make out what they were saying. To be honest, I was worried that something bad was going to happen. David's parents were divorced, and he spent some time with his Dad but lived with his Mom. He said it was okay, but he missed his dad a lot of the time. I don't know how I fell asleep with so much worry in the air but I did.

▪

When Mom woke me up in the morning, I hadn't even gotten under the covers. "How are you Tommy?" she asked.

"Okay."

"You sure?"

I nodded. "Is Dad okay?"

She nodded back. "He's feeling real sad about Uncle Aaron."

"I'm sad, too."

"I'm sure you are. But sometimes a person just needs to let some feelings out. Dad's not going to work today. He's gonna stay home and try to feel better. You should work on your school stuff and take care of Ella."

"Okay."

When Mom left, I got up and looked out the window. The dawn light was glowing on the top of the leaf gone trees. Dad was just standing in the driveway looking into the garage. He had a couple of band aids on the fingers of his right hand. I guess that was from when he was trying to pick up the pieces of broken glass.

■

We were out of school for another few days. I took Ella to the park. Kareem was there. Even though it was cold, he was shooting baskets and dribbling around. He let me shoot a couple and then I started passing the ball to him to set up some three pointers. Ella watched for a while, then got bored and wandered off.

"How was Christmas?" I asked Kareem.

"Good. I gave Latitia two of those perfume things you gave me. She loved that, man. Thanks. It was perfect for her. She's all about style."

"She always looks good. Now she smells good," I said.

Kareem shot a three pointer from the side. It swished.

"I got Assassins Creed III for Christmas," he announced.

"Cool."

"Maybe we can get together and try it out," he suggested.

"Yeah. That would be great." I could hear Ella calling me. She was down by the creek. "I'm babysitting."

"She's not a baby anymore," Kareem said.

"Not according to my Mom. See ya."

"Yeah. Don't forget Assassins Creed," he yelled back at me.

"I won't."

In the old days, a couple of years ago, Kareem and I hung out a lot. His uncle even took me fishing one day in the country. We'd play video games and some-times practice baseball. We'd just toss the ball or go to the playground and play Hit the Bat. Just warming up for the season. But Kareem wouldn't be playing baseball anymore. When spring came he'd run track to get in shape for basketball camps in the summer. So chances were we wouldn't be playing Assassins Creed anytime soon.

I trotted over to the stream. Ella pointed at some small fish. Her face looked sad. She didn't seem like her old self.

"What's wrong?" I asked.

"I don't know."

"Come on. Something's bothering you."

"Last night. The yelling. It was awful. It scared me,"

Ella said, not looking right at me.

"I don't think you should worry about it now. It's over."

I could tell she didn't believe me. I was scared and worried too and she could feel that. It would take time to get over the feelings. We walked home, not talking or joking. Suddenly, she wanted to race, and we ran the last two blocks. She won. Like I say, she's really fast.

When we reached the house, we saw a silver X5 in the driveway. Ella looked at me.

"I don't know who it is," I said.

We eased up to the kitchen window and looked inside. Mr. Grady, Dad's boss, was sitting at the table with Mom and Dad. Was Dad getting fired for missing work today? They'd been drinking coffee. I was about to bolt in the door when I saw them bow their heads. Mr. Grady was saying a prayer.

"What are they doing?" Ella whispered.

"They're praying."

"For what?" she asked.

"You don't have to pray for anything. You can just pray." Mignon's words were ringing in my head.

After the prayer, Mr. Grady got up and gave Mom a hug and then he looked at Dad and shook his still bandaged hand. Dad nodded and then Mr. Grady gave him a hug too. Mr. Grady was a real big man. I wouldn't call him fat but he was large in every way. Big head and big hands. He could hug you to death.

Ella and I walked into the house.

"Hey, sport. How's it going?" Mr. Grady said.

"Good. Real good."

"Have a nice Christmas?"

"Yes, sir."

"And Ella, you're getting bigger every day."

"Yeah, I know. Half my clothes don't fit anymore."

"I know that feeling," Mr. Grady said, patting his stomach. He looked to Mom. "Well, I've got to be going. Nice to see you, Claire. And Rick I'll see you Tuesday."

"It's a deal," Dad said.

Mom was smiling, and she put on her apron to start making dinner. Dad went to the garage to do some more work on that Norton. Ella and I stood there for a minute, confused. We knew something had happened between the grownups but we weren't sure what it was.

▪

For New Year's we went downtown for the celebration. Ella wore the sunglasses I gave her, even though it was night. Dad wore a State sweat shirt and Mom gave herself a little spray of Madagascar. Understand, when I smelled that cologne I thought of Mignon. I could see her smile and the way she stood with one hip out when she was studying you. It would have been nice if she could have come with us, but her family was having a party at their house for relatives and friends.

There was a good crowd downtown for the early festivities. I ate a good taco. Dad had a hot dog with chili. Ella tried to ice skate on the little rink they'd set up.

"How can you see with those sunglasses on?" Mom asked her.

"I can see good. It's brighter than you think."

That was about when she ran into an Asian boy, who was already spinning for a fall. That made her hit the wall with a thud and she flopped onto the ice. She was okay (Ella's tough) and she started laughing as soon as she got back up on her skates.

In the middle of the main street they had set up a stage where a couple of bands took turns playing. Mom tried to get me to dance, but I dodged her.

"Are you embarrassed to dance with your mom?" she asked.

"No way," I fibbed. "Not my kind of music."

So she grabbed Dad and she got him to hip shake a little and do some old dance they call the shag. He wasn't really into it, but he tried. "This is my dad's move," he said, and spun Mom around and dipped her almost to the ground. That was the first time I'd seen him smile since before the funeral. And Mom was smiling, too. They looked pretty silly but nice too.

Finally Mom decided to eat something, and found a cart selling gyros. Ella only wanted sweets, so she got a doughnut. At nine—early, so little kids wouldn't have to stay out late—the countdown started. I always liked fireworks and these were just terrific. There were whirling ones that spun above the trees and then big bursting flowery ones that blew up in wild colors. Rockets went up and filled the sky with light. They seemed to go on forever, right over our heads. The booms bounced off the tall buildings and made some of the smaller kids hold their ears. Then came the big finale of everything at once. Red, green, gold, and silver sparks rained all around. Kids yelled. People stopped whatever they were doing and stared at the show. It was great, even if it was a little early.

"Happy New Year, Dad!" Ella shouted, and Dad grabbed her and gave her a squeeze. You could smell the gunpowder or whatever it was in the air. We all gave each other a hug without saying a word.

Once I was in bed I didn't want to sleep until it really was the new year. I got Mignon on FaceTime and she said she'd call back before 12 and we'd count down together. I could hear the voices and music in the background of the party at her house. I had half dozed off when she buzzed me. It was exactly 11:59.

"Are you asleep?" she asked.

"Almost."

"We're best friends, aren't we?"

"I hope so," I said.

"FaceTime."

I clicked on and her face gleamed like the moon.

"Let's count down together, okay?"

"Starting when?"

"At ten. I've got the TV in my room on and I can see Times Square in New York City, where they drop the ball. Can you see?" She tilted the lens. I could see it in the corner of her room.

"You start."

There was a long pause. I saw the gleaming ball as it slowly fell.

"Ten, nine, eight, seven." We were in sync. "Three, two, one." Fireworks went off in the distance.

"Happy New Year, Mignon."

"Happy New Year, Tommy. And good night."

"Sleep tight."

"Don't let the bed bugs bite," she whispered.

A kiss on the screen and then she was gone. This was the happiest I'd felt in a long time. I relaxed against my cool pillow and pulled the covers up. The fireworks were still exploding in our neighborhood. It was probably the Jenkins kids. They were in high school and liked to do stunts. A couple of rockets went off nearby. I could hear the swoosh and the boom and then a burning sound. The sky was lit for a few seconds as the sparks drifted down and fell among the pines, and then I fell asleep in the newest year.

CHAPTER NINE

A FEW NIGHTS LATER, I got the star map that Mignon had given me and snuck out of the house. It was the first time I'd done that but I was more excited than nervous. It was really cold, but the sky was clear. I headed for the baseball field at the end of the park. It was a good place to check the stars—without a lot of trees hiding the sky. I could stand on the pitcher's mound and search, using the map.

First I found the North Star. Then I could see the Big Dipper and then the constellation they call Gemini, the twins. Two bright stars. That was pretty easy. Then, using my new phone as a flashlight, I checked the map. I looked for other constellations, like Taurus and Orion. Was that the Little Dipper over there, near the North Star?

Doing this, I couldn't help but think of those ancient people, looking at the skies and trying to figure out what was going on. They didn't have big, powerful telescopes and satellites or star maps. They just had their eyes. But they had questions, like me. They wanted to know where they were and who they were and what was controlling everything. I mean, they had a lot of gods—gods for different things. But I don't know if that helped when they looked at the sky and saw the twinkling, moving stars and the bright moon, waxing and waning. They still had their questions, and their gods were silent.

After a while the wind picked up and some clouds rolled in and the stars disappeared. By the time I reached my street, small snowflakes were falling. I could see them in the streetlight. I remembered that my fifth-grade teacher had told us that no two snowflakes are alike. If that's true, snowflakes are a lot like people.

When I got home, it was dead quiet. I tiptoed very slowly to my room when suddenly Ella jumped out from behind her door and spooked me. "Dang, Ella, don't do that. My heart almost stopped."

"Where were you?" she whispered.

"Out."

"Doing what?" she asked.

"Looking at the stars."

"By yourself?"

"Yeah. Don't tell Mom," I begged.

She looked at me long and hard. I don't know if she believed me.

"You're crazy," she said. Maybe she was right. Maybe I was becoming a little crazy.

"It's snowing," I told her.

"I don't believe you," she said, and went back to bed without looking through any window at the falling flakes.

That Saturday I was playing a video game downstairs when Dad walked in, holding baseball gloves. It was sunny outside and not so cold. We went in the yard and just started tossing. Easy throws at first and then we got more distance, so we could put some sizzle on the ball. Dad has a good arm and can even throw a knuckler. We did this kind of throwing practice each year before baseball season.

"We should go to the batting cage a few times before you start practicing, just to work on your eye and your timing," Dad said.

"That would be great."

I made a low throw, which he dropped. He picked up the ball and stopped, as if he had a pain in his arm. But the pain wasn't in his arm.

"Tommy," he said, "I want to apologize for what happened with Mom after Christmas." He looked deep into me.

"That's okay."

"No, it isn't. It was bad. I disappointed myself, and I'm sure I scared you and Ella. But I'm really sorry. And I hope to make up for it."

I didn't know what to say, and neither did he. He just walked deeper into the yard, turned, and tossed the ball to me again. We played catch for another fifteen minutes or so and then he went back into the garage to work on the Norton some more. I felt sorry that he still felt so bad. I wished I could have made him feel better, but maybe I did, by listening and throwing. I hope he knows that

I don't think anybody's perfect; that's why, in church, people ask for forgiveness all the time and usually get it.

■

The story I had written for class before Christmas came back to me the second week of the new semester. Miss Tyler had drawn a huge A on it. That was a great grade because Miss Tyler is very particular and strict. She has a big black mole on her right cheek and when she is angry it appears to twitch. Today there was no twitching. After she handed back everybody's stories and poems, she faced the class.

"Well, students, I want to commend all of you for your work on this creative project. I especially want to congratulate Emily Perkins for her poem called "Spring in My Backyard" and Thomas Johnson for his story, "Pier Fishing." Emily isn't here today—I think she has the flu. But Thomas is here and I'd like for him to read some of his story to you."

She hadn't warned me, and I was freaking. Micky kicked my desk and Mignon gave me a smile. I felt kind of jittery and wanted to pee.

"Don't be shy, Thomas," Miss Tyler said. She motioned me to come up. I took a breath and walked to her desk.

"You just want me to start reading it?" I asked.

"Yes, but turn around and face the class."

I could hear Mignon's laugh as I turned. I couldn't look at anybody, so I kept my eyes on the page and read the story, like she told me to. It's no use to repeat it here. It was about a young boy (could be me) going fishing for the first time with his dad from a pier at the beach. After a bunch of nibbles, the boy catches a fish—a red drum. He has mixed feelings about catching the fish when some of the other fishermen tell him it will be good eating. His dad, sensing the boy's feelings, releases the fish back into the water where it is free to swim away. That makes the boy happy. That was the gist of it.

"Is that enough?" I asked.

"Yes, Thomas. Thank you."

Before I could scoot back to my desk, Micky and Mignon started clapping, which kind of forced the other people to clap. Dave whistled and hooted, like I'd scored a touchdown, and that got a big glare from Miss Tyler. I didn't mind the attention, to be honest, but I didn't want to dwell on it.

At lunch, Mignon nudged me as I was chomping down on a hot dog. "That was good. The story. What I heard of it."

"Thanks," I said. "What did you write about?"

"I wrote a poem about my dog, Pierre. It was kind of stupid."

"What did you get?"

"She gave me a B, and I was thrilled. My spelling sucks. I'm not a writer like you."

Another sort of compliment.

"When does soccer start?" I asked.

"Next month, I think."

"That's good."

"Why do you always change the subject?" she asked, scrunching up her face.

"Sorry."

"Can I read your story some time?"

I nodded just as the bell rang and the stampede to class started. I could tell Mignon was impressed. It reminded me that I'd had felt a similar feeling about her when she showed me a drawing she'd done of a swan. She'd made the feathers look very real. But the best part was that she had put a moon behind the swan, and the moonlight looked like it was shimmering on the lake.

■

I think you should know something about Mignon's dog, Pierre, because he had a big effect on my relationship with Mignon. Pierre is a medium- sized dog and at first, because of his name, I thought he might be a poodle, but it turned out he was something called a Kerry Blue Terrier. Funny. He wasn't blue at all but black and curly. I met Mignon in sixth grade and sometimes in those early days I'd go by her house. Every time I knocked on her front door, Pierre would sneak behind me and give me a good nip on the butt. He never barked. He just eased up the steps and nipped me. After a while, I would be ready for him and right before I knocked on the door, I'd turn around real quick and see him standing there staring at me. He didn't back off or wag his tail or anything. He just stared with those big black eyes. I could tell he didn't like me, and he was just waiting for me to let my guard down. When I did—like I'd come in the kitchen and Mignon would offer me a cookie or something—I'd forget Pierre was around, and sure enough, he'd get me. The point of this story is that whenever I went to see Mignon at her house, it was a big deal. You'd have to want to see someone a lot to put up with Pierre's nips. I think Mignon saw that as a test of our friendship.

▪

The Valentine's dance was a big middle-school deal—mainly to the girls, but a few of the eighth-grade boys were getting into it, too. The theme this year was Midnight in Paris, even though the dance would be over by 10, at the latest. Mignon was on the dance committee; they'd spent more than a week on the decorations. Mignon's mom helped out, along with several other parents. (She looks a little like Mignon—same color eyes and hair, but Mignon is already as tall as her, and thinner.) In the middle of the gym there was a cardboard Eiffel Tower. It was about as tall as Kareem. They had chairs and little tables, with empty wine bottles on them set off to one side. It was supposed to be like a Paris cafe. Against the back wall, pictures of Paris were being projected: a bridge over the river; a cathedral; a park with a rose garden; a view up a big avenue to a giant arch. Pretty interesting. French flags were just about everywhere, and of course, it being Valentine's, hearts decorated everything else. The deejay was wearing a striped shirt and a beret which was supposed to make him look French. He'd also put on a fake mustache, which he seemed not to like very much. He kept adjusting it.

Only a few people had dates. Kareem came with Latitia. Nancy Forester came with Vince Jordan and his sister, Lana. Nancy didn't pay much attention to Vince, because she was on the lookout for Dimon. They were the only ones you could say had actual dates. Everybody else was doing solo. There were clumps of boys and girls waiting for something to happen. Mignon had come with Jeannie. She was dressed up in a very pink dress and black sort of high-heel shoes. Her hair was piled up on her head and she was wearing gold earrings. I had never seen her like that. Almost grown-up. She looked more than pretty: I think she looked beautiful.

When the music started, it was a slow-go at first. Kareem slid out on the floor with Latitia and led the way; then Ralph went out with Hannah Hempstead. Maria Papadopoulos and Grant looked like a couple.

I'm not much of a dancer. I can hop and jostle like a zombie or something. I have rhythm and I love music, but I don't know any real dances. That doesn't seem to bother Micky; he makes up his own dances to whatever music is playing.

After 20 minutes and two sodas and a cupcake, I went out on the floor with a group including Mignon and Jeannie and Lana Jordan and I can't remember who else, because my attention was fixed on Mignon. After about five out-of-control minutes to the Granules' "Don't Stop Me", I was starting to sweat. We retreated to the tables. Mignon was still swaying with the beat.

"You look terrific," I finally said.

"Thank you. But I think I'm going to need to take off these shoes," she said, pulling her foot from one of the shoes and stretching her toes.

"I guess it's hard to dance in them."

"Sort of. I should have just worn flats or my Converses."

Suddenly, there was a change in the music. The deejay had put on a slow one—you know, one of those Taylor Swift ones. I saw Dimon take Nancy by the hand and pull her close. Some eighth graders were squeezing together. A few grinders got going. Miss Tyler and Mr. Henkel, the dance monitors for the night, looked nervous and concerned.

"You want to dance?" Mignon asked me.

I shrugged. "I don't think so."

"Come on."

I shook my head.

"What's the matter?" she asked.

I couldn't answer. "I got to pee."

She looked at me with her head cocked to one side. I really did have to pee, so I headed for the bathroom at the end of the gym. I was really feeling stupid—like a coward, and I know that's how I must have seemed to her. The thing is, I didn't know how to slow-dance. Or did I just not know how to hold a girl close? What if I threw another boner? It's so random. I would have given anything to be out there with Mignon, looking so pretty. Why was I scared? If I stumbled around, would she care? I took a long, slow pee, which was a relief, and was washing my hands at the sink when Micky came in.

"You better watch it, bro," he said.

"Watch what?"

He was peeing now.

"Clay Harris, the Third."

"What are you talking about?"

"You got to check your radar. After you left, he put on his cool look and walked over. Nudged in with that phony grin of his. Jeannie went all fluttery."

"And?"

"He asked Mignon to dance, I guess, because that's what they're doing."

My face felt flushed. I was suddenly a wreck.

"A slow dance?" I asked.

"Yeah."

"Well, it's a free country," I said trying to stay cool, but my knees were weak.

Guess I'd better tell you about Clay Harris, the Third. He's an eighth grader. And that means there was a Clay Harris Junior and a just plain Clay Harris. Clay, the Third is a basketball star and captain of the lacrosse team. His parents own a software company, so they have a lot of money, or so everybody thinks. He always has the greatest kicks. Some European-only Adidas or something. He always seems to be smiling, and why not? He's tall and, according to most of the girls in the school, very handsome. No pimples anywhere. He's hit on almost every girl in the eighth grade and a few in the seventh.

Micky's news was depressing. I didn't want to go back to the gym and see him with Mignon in his arms. That would make me sick.

As Micky turned to go, he said, "You better get out there. I mean if you care."

"I will. Don't worry." But I stayed in the bathroom for a few more minutes and tried to think that none of this mattered, with the vast universe hovering over us, but then Clay Harris, the Third walked in.

"Hey, Tommy," he said. "How's it going?"

"Good. Good."

"These dances are so damn boring, aren't they?" he asked, shaking his big head.

"You said it."

"But the girls like it. They like to dress up and look hot. So we have to show them that we notice."

"That's a fact. So obvious." My voice didn't sound real.

He laughed and unzipped. Even his pee was powerful. It sounded like a waterfall as it hit the urinal. I wanted to leave.

"Well, see you," I mumbled.

"By the way. That Mignon. She's a friend of yours, right?"

"Yeah." I was scared of what he might say. Would I have to attack him and be beaten to a pulp?

"She's really cute," he said.

"You think so?"

"Smoking." He used stupid slang from movies. "She's really grown up this year."

"Yeah. She blossomed…like a…tulip."

Clay Harris, the Third laughed until he almost choked. What a lame thing to say. Tulip.

"You sure got a way with words, bud."

I couldn't say anymore. I couldn't hear anymore. My heart was pounding. When he started washing his hands, I left the bathroom and edged back out to the dance floor. I didn't see Mignon at first. Micky was having his sixth soda. (His parents forbid soda in their house.) The deejay was playing a song by the Killers and a crowd went out to dance together. When I finally spotted Mignon, she was in the corner with Jeannie and Lana and Nancy and they were laughing and gossiping. She didn't notice me. I started hopping around next to Brenda Banks, from my math class.

"Great dance," she shouted.

I just nodded. I wanted to leave, but instead something strange took over my brain. I started doing a crazy dance, which I made up to the beat of the song, just like Micky. I was whirling around and jumping and stomping and the sweat was beading up under my shirt. While I was spinning, I could occasionally see Mignon and then Clay Harris, the Third, came into view and I just danced harder and kept spinning and I knew I was getting dizzy but I couldn't stop. In that space between the end of one song and the beginning of another, I stumbled like a drunk and crashed into the Eiffel Tower and knocked it over.

"Whoa, cowboy!" I heard someone yell. Was it Clay? Micky and me and Sid Davenport picked up the Eiffel Tower and set it straight. I felt like such a dork. The deejay—whose mustache had fallen off—played another song and everybody started bouncing again. Without looking anywhere in particular, I stumbled to the side door and into the cold night air. The stars were out as usual, looking down on me, helping me to feel even smaller and dumber. Almost invisible. I called home and Dad said he'd pick me up. While I was waiting and shivering, I could hear another slow dance starting. I really hated that. I imagined Mignon in her pink dress taking off her shoes to dance with Clay Harris the Third.

It was a Justin Bieber song, every line mocking me: "That should be me, that should be me." As much as I hate Bieber, I hope you stop reading here and play the song. Then you'll know how low I felt, waiting for Dad's truck to pull up. Sappy lyrics. Sappy me.

"That should be me, feeling your kiss. That should be me…"

▪

At school the next week I kind of avoided Mignon for a few days. Even at lunch, sitting at the same table with her, I didn't say much. She'd try to talk but I wouldn't take the bait. At the end of the day, instead of walking with her and Kareem I'd hang around school. One day I worked with Coach Wrenn on some infield pointers and drills. He was surprised that I was putting in the time. "It's gonna pay dividends for you, Johnson, when the season starts." Coaches say stuff like that all the time.

That Friday, Mignon grabbed me by the sleeve as I was heading out to do a campus cleanup project with some other volunteers. Half of them were on disciplinary probation.

"What's the matter with you?" she asked. She seemed upset.

"What do you mean?"

"You know what I mean."

I did, and I must have blushed. "Look, I got to go do

this project."

"I'll wait," she said. And that's what she did. After I dumped my trash bag in the recycle bin, I saw her sitting on the entrance steps. She followed me inside while I got my backpack. The hall was empty.

"Ever since the dance you've been weird," Mignon said, walking towards me.

"You think?"

"Don't b.s. me." She was getting angry.

"Don't make it such a big deal."

She came closer, making me look at her. "What's the matter?" she asked.

"I just feel stupid," I said.

"About what?"

A word was floating up in my brain and I couldn't say it at first. I'd never ever used the word before.

"Say something. Don't be a coward."

That stung. I could feel the anger twisting in me and knew it was just because I was embarrassed.

"Look. I think I was jealous."

The word fell out of my mouth like a stone. Mignon gave me a wrinkled nose look.

"Jealous? Why?"

"You know."

"No, I don't," she said.

"When I heard you were dancing with Clay."

She snorted. "Is that what this is all about?"

"No. It's about me, and how I felt. I know it's dumb. I just freaked."

For some reason, she smiled.

"Why are you smiling?" I asked.

"Because it's kind of sweet."

I took a deep breath. My little whirlwind of anger started to disappear.

"He's a god to all you girls."

"Not to me. He's too full of himself. He just wants you to tell him how cool he is. That's so uncool."

"You danced with him."

"I like to dance. I asked you first."

"I don't really know how."

"You certainly were doing something with Brenda."

She'd noticed. I was feeling better.

"That wasn't real dancing."

"Then you disappeared after the Eiffel Tower fell over. I thought you got sick or something."

"Well. I kind of did."

She looked at me for a long moment. I think she was sizing me up, trying to figure out how she really felt about me.

"Let's go home," she said.

We walked for a long time without talking. When we got to the park, Kareem was already there, playing three on three with some older guys. He waved.

"Kareem was looking for you at the dance. I told him I didn't know what happened."

I turned to her. "If I knew how to dance...slow, I would have danced with you. That's for sure."

She stopped for a moment. "Does anybody in your family dance?" she asked.

"Sometimes my parents do this old dance, swinging

around. But not very often."

She stood still for another moment, then tugged my sleeve. "C'mon."

"Where?"

"My house."

"I can't. I need to get home."

"Just call your mom."

I knew Mom would be okay with it. She was busy. She'd be in the dining room with the doors closed, practically day and night. Tax season had started and she was busy at her work. I figured we'd probably have to order pizza that night.

After I called Mom, Mignon and I headed to her house. Her mom was home and must have been doing laundry, because she had a big basket of clothes in her arms. For once Pierre seemed happy to see me, but I didn't trust him.

"You know Tommy," Mignon said to her mom who was holding a basket of laundry.

"Yes, of course. Hi, Tommy."

"Hello, Mrs. Eubanks."

"I'm gonna teach him to dance."

Mrs. Eubanks smiled. "That's a great idea," she said.

With that, Mignon pulled open a door that led downstairs to a den her folks had built in the basement. I'd never been down those steps. There was nice wood paneling in the room and a bar with stools. By the bar was a football jersey from LSU in a frame. A ping-pong table was in the middle of the floor.

"This is weird," I said.

"Help me fold this up," Mignon asked, ignoring my protest.

We took down the net and folded the table in half. Then we rolled it into a corner.

"I'm not sure this is gonna work," I said. I remembered how tough the agility drills had been for football.

"That's not a good attitude."

It was obvious that Mignon was enjoying herself. She plugged in an old boom box, searched through a stack of CDs and found what she was looking for. "What kind of music do you like?" she asked.

"Most everything, but not the slow-dance stuff," I answered.

"Well, that's what's freaking you out."

The music started. A girl was singing about breaking up with someone. I'd heard the song before on the radio, but I usually changed the station.

"Put your hands here," she ordered, guiding my hands to her waist.

"You don't have to squeeze," she added.

"Sorry." I was a little nervous.

She laughed and then she put her hands on my shoulders. I felt stiff and awkward.

"Just go with the beat," she said.

"I don't know...."

She stopped. "You said you would have danced with me if you knew how. Right?"

"Yeah."

"Well, this is all there is to it. Relax."

She slowly rocked me side to side and showed me

some steps. Actually, it was pretty easy. I shuffled. She shuffled. The music had a sad feeling, with violins and stuff. She put her head on my shoulder. I pulled her a little closer. It was getting really warm. She smelled like flowers and sweat. Sweet and sour. I closed my eyes for a second and felt my arms relax. The music finally stopped.

"See. That's all you need to do."

I couldn't look at her face for more than a second. "Not bad," I said.

"One more time?" she asked.

"Okay."

We danced to the song again. It was easier and I even gave her a spin as the song ended, like I saw on "Dancing with the Stars" one time.

"Want to practice some more?" Mignon asked.

"No. I think I got it."

"See? Next time there's a dance you have no excuse."

"I guess so."

Honestly, I wanted to kiss her right there and I think she wouldn't have been surprised, either. But her Mom called her to dinner and I realized that I had to get home, too. So I just gave her a quick hug.

"See you later." I sprinted down the steps with Pierre right behind. I could hear the click of his pointy teeth as he nipped at me.

"You missed!" I yelled as I cleared the porch.

I ran home all the way, with my backpack bouncing. When I banged through the back door, Ella was watching a TV show and Jake was sleeping with his legs in the air. Mom stepped out of the dining room and gave me a look.

. "What have you been doing?" she asked.

"Dancing," I said, and headed for my room. The look on Mom's face was priceless.

Before bed I had some FaceTime with Mignon and thanked her for the lesson. At least for this one night I didn't think about any galaxies or mind-boggling black holes but only about how good it felt to have her so close and in my arms.

Dancing. Who knew?

CHAPTER TEN

FEBRUARY HAD A couple of other events of note before it ended. The Tar Heels beat Duke 74 to 66 in Chapel Hill. That warmed me up against the cold. Then David brought the Sports Illustrated Swim Suit Issue to school which caused a major commotion in the parking lot when he pulled it out of his backpack. Everybody wanted to get a peek. He was lucky it wasn't torn up in the scrum before he could stow it in his locker. His dad would have been very angry had that happened.

"I'll never do this again," David said and that was understandable.

The middle-school spring sport season started just as the first daffodils poked up from the ground. Mignon was out with the girls' soccer team and I showed up for baseball. I wanted to keep playing second base. I didn't like being in the outfield. You just stood there most of the game. Every now and then a ball would come out there and you had to jump into action. If you had a tendency to daydream, which I did, you sometimes were caught off guard. And I didn't have a real strong arm, which was another problem. In any case, being in the infield, you felt more into the game. You were chatting it up with everybody and concentrating on the hitter and the situation. You didn't have time to daydream, so you were always on your toes.

Thankfully Coach Wrenn put me back at second and moved the new red-headed kid, Sean MacDonald, to right where I was usually stuck when I was in the outfield.. Sean's a pretty good guy. He'd moved here from New York, from some town near Canada. His Dad got a new job in the research park. Sean's voice is kind of high-pitched, and he talks real fast.

"You get a little dash of snow down here and you guys freak out. It's funny," he said, leaning on the fence waiting to bat. "We get snow all winter. Eventually it starts freezing. Even the rivers freeze over."

"You're kidding?"

"Nope. Where I used to live, when the winter starts for real they string these barrels across the river that make a net to keep the ice from going into the electric plant. You know, the hydroelectric plant?"

"Yeah, I've heard of them things," I said, with a real country accent. Sean laughed and snorted.

"Over the winter, big clumps of ice pack up against the net, like a wall, higher and thicker. We go out there and slide around. Cops are always chasing us off."

"How tall is it?" I asked.

"It's tall. It's like a building or like a cliff. Yeah, like a big, white cliff. And it's long. All winter it builds and builds."

Randy Parker hit a foul ball that zipped over our heads. Sean didn't seem to notice. "You know how we know it's spring up there?"

I shook my head.

"They go out on the ice and remove all the barrels and traps and nets. And then, because it's really thick, they have to blow the ice up with dynamite to get the river flowing again. Huge explosions. Pow! Big chunks of ice go flying in the air. When the ice breaks up and the river starts flowing, people cheer like at a big game. It's spring again."

"I'd like to see that," I said.

"Yeah, it's something to see. So what you call winter down here is a joke."

"MacDonald," Coach Wrenn called. "You're up."

Sean got in the cage and took some hefty cuts but didn't really blast anything.

"I got a little shoulder problem, Coach. Going to the doctor tomorrow."

"You were a little impatient, is all. Just relax up there," Coach Wrenn said, and tapped his temple.

I think Sean was just nervous, being the new guy, a long way from home.

Our spring was an explosion, too. The fruit trees bloomed overnight and the dogwoods were ready to pop. Every yard seemed to have a dogwood or a redbud. Grass was growing again and the trees were full of new leaves. Birds were chirping. Even the dogs seemed to be in a better mood. Was I gonna get spring fever? What is that anyway? You hear about it, but what exactly is it?

■

Our first game was against Copeland. We won, four to two. I got an infield hit and didn't strike out once, which was a breakthrough for me. I made two good plays on grounders and one dumb play on a little pop-up, which bounced off my glove. Mom came to the game even though she was in the middle of her tax work. She gave me a big hug when it was over. Micky was there too, but Mignon had soccer practice.

With all the practices starting at the same time, you didn't see your friends as often as you liked. Mignon loved soccer, and sometimes if we had a break I'd go over and watch her play from a hill behind the soccer field. She's fast. Because she has a long stride, it doesn't seem like she's trying at all, but you can see that the girls with shorter legs have to churn to keep up with her. And when she nails the ball it's really rocked. One of her shots hit Natalie Lowdowski in the stomach, and she crumpled like she'd been gunned down. Everybody ran over to help her, including Mignon, who seemed really worried. It turned out she'd only had the wind knocked out; in a few minutes she was back up and playing.

"That shot on Natalie was a blast," I said to her in the park later.

"I didn't mean to hurt her." Mignon had picked a dogwood blossom and put it in her hair.

"How does this look?" she asked.

"Good. A little bit country and little bit rock and roll."

"Maybe I'll get a chance to see one of your games next

week," she said.

"See me in action. Yeah, that should thrill you."

"Why do you always put yourself down?" she asked like she was annoyed with me.

"Just dealing with reality."

She shook her head.

"I think you're fishing for compliments," she said. "That sort of reverse thing, where you say, 'Oh, I'm so bad' and then someone has to say, 'No you're great' Is it like that?"

"Maybe, but what does it matter? When I read the obituaries. . . ."

"You still into that?" she interrupted.

"Yeah, of course."

She scrunched her face up. "You're obsessed."

"It's very educational. I recommend it."

She shook her head and fast-pitched a pinecone at me. I picked up a stubby branch and asked her to throw another one. When she did, I smacked it over her head and into the creek.

"Good swing."

"I'd be a star in the pinecone league."

Her phone buzzed. She picked up.

"I'm in the park with Tommy. No, we are not. Shut up." She pocketed her phone.

"We're not what?"

"Nothing. Tell me what you've read in the obituaries that's so interesting."

"Well, just this week, there was a write-up for somebody who died 20 years ago, and they were saying happy birthday. He would have been 86. They had his picture in there, smiling. His family hadn't forgotten him."

"That's nice. What else?"

"There was Otis Brown, a Double-A man, who was 78. Worked at the sanitation department for 36 years before he retired. Loved to hunt and fish. Big Tar Heel fan. Left two children and six grandchildren."

"Did he have a photo?" she asked.

"No. Not everybody gets one. I don't know how that works or if there's a limit to how much you can say. The one with the best picture was Sandra Oates of Smithfield. She died at 82, but the picture of her was from when she was young and real pretty. Graduated from Sweet Briar College, in Virginia. She married a lawyer, Wilfred Oates. Instead of flowers she wanted people to send money to Hospice House of Johnston County or the Red Cross."

"Does it ever say what they died from?"

"Nope. Not usually."

"Well, Mrs. Oates was old. Maybe she just stopped living."

"Yeah, but I've seen some young ones in the paper too. Like last week, there was this guy who went to Apex High School. He was fourteen and he died. He played trumpet in the band. Who knows how he died? Accident, some weird disease. The truth is you never know."

"Sad," she said.

"How about my Uncle Aaron? Out for a ride, enjoying himself and bang. He's gone. Just like that. I mean, a big branch could fall off one of these trees and hit me in the head and kill me right now. Just like that."

Mignon looked up at the branches of those big oaks and old pines that hovered over us. "One could hit me, too."

"Yeah, that's what I'm saying. When you walk through a cemetery, and look at those old graves and think of all the people there, they were as alive as you and me. Some died old; some died young. Some were good and some were bad."

She shook her head. "You know something, Tommy? You're totally strange."

"Really?"

"Why do you think I like you?" She was sort of smiling, so I guess strange was good. We ambled back to our bikes. She didn't say much. She pulled some gum out of her pocket and offered me some. Usually I'm not into gum but I took it. It had kind of a tropical fruit taste.

"You know, I've never been to a cemetery," she said finally.

"What about when your grandmother died?"

"She was cremated. We just had a memorial service at the church."

"Well, I haven't been to that many myself. But there's one over by the shopping center, a small one. We could just walk over there one day," I suggested.

"And do what?"

"Just look around."

She didn't say yes or no. She got on her bike and pedaled off. "Don't forget to study," she reminded me, as usual.

I did study that night. Around nine o'clock I heard

Dad fire up the Norton for a few minutes. It was running high and sputtering. After a few minutes, when the engine got warm, the sound got more even. It was real loud, because there wasn't any muffler on the exhaust, and when Dad cut the engine, there was a big backfire.

"Getting close, damn it!" he yelled to Mom. "Real close." There was a little of the old fire in his voice.

■

I went to see Mignon play soccer one afternoon, after school. They were playing Wilson. Mignon made a good pass to Brenda Banks for the first goal. The girls were jumping around more than the boys ever do. Mrs. Eubanks was there cheering for them. I figured the tall man next to her was Mr. Eubanks. When I went over to say hello, Mrs. Eubanks gave me a big smile and a hug.

"Tommy, have you ever met my husband, Maurice?"

"No, ma'am. Nice to meet you, sir."

I stuck out my hand and he gave it a good shake.

"I've heard a lot about you from Mignon and Paulette," he said. "Nice to finally meet you."

"He's the one she taught to dance," Mrs. Eubanks told him. From the look on his face, I think he already knew.

I didn't know quite what to say about the dancing, so I changed the subject. "Mignon's playing real good," I said.

"Yes, but she drifts a little."

"I do, too."

"You play a sport?" he asked.

"Yes, sir. Baseball right now."

"I loved playing baseball. What position do you play?"

"Second base."

"I was stupid enough to be a catcher," Mr. Eubanks said, shaking his head. He held up his right hand so I could see that the little finger was bent in a weird angle. "And my index finger on this other hand won't bend at all."

He sighed. Mrs. Eubanks shook her head and I took that as my clue to move on.

"Well, nice to meet you," I said and waved myself away.

I could see Micky and David sitting in the bleachers.

"Want to get a smoothie?" Micky asked me.

He wanted to go down to the smoothie shop on the corner. Debbie Jurgenson, this high school girl, worked there. She had major breasts.

"I don't feel like a smoothie today," I said.

He shrugged. "Your girlfriend's playing good."

"She's not my girlfriend."

"She's a girl and she's a friend. That's all I'm saying." Of course, that wasn't all he was saying.

After the game, Micky and David went to the smoothie store and I waited for Mignon. She gave her backpack to her parents and walked over to where I was sitting.

"Are you walking?" she asked.

"Yeah."

"I'll walk with you." She waved at her mom to let her know they could go home without her. We started down Maple and headed past the Taco Bell.

"You played great today."

"Thanks."

"Met your Dad today. He seems nice."

"He is nice. He's, well, he's my dad. How's your dad?"

"Getting better, I think." I'd had told her a little bit about the incident. We walked another block. "You want to see that cemetery?"

She gave me a long look. "Okay. Sure."

We had to walk six blocks out of our way and then turn down a driveway between two buildings and past a couple of dumpsters. You could hardly see the cemetery. It was hidden by the dumpsters and a bunch of wild hedges. We pushed through the hedges and suddenly there we were. The cemetery went downhill under some old water oaks. Wild wisteria was already blooming on the edge of the lot and vines like giant snakes grew around some of the trees. There was a group of headstones just as you entered with the name "Simmons" chiseled on them. The first date of death we could read was 1888. Mignon bent down to see if she could scrape away some of the moss on the stone, but the old letters had been worn down.

"I wonder why this place is just sitting here in the middle of all these buildings," Mignon said, cleaning the dirt from her hands.

"Well, I think there's some kind of law that you can't build on top of a cemetery. So I guess when they started building all around here they had to leave the dead people where they were."

"How did you find it?" she asked.

"One day David and I were just goofing, trying to hide from Micky. We ran back here."

Mignon looked at another marker. "Here's one from

1911: Mabel Turner. Born in 1840. That would make her 71 when she died."

"Good math," I said.

A stone angel that had marked a grave had toppled over and was now covered in purple wisteria blossoms. Mignon pointed to a place near a hedge. "There's only one grave here with any flowers, and they're plastic and really old and nasty."

"When I was at my uncle's funeral, I kept thinking while I was walking in the cemetery, here are all these people in old graves where nobody visits anymore. They're forgotten. Gone, and after some time, anybody who knew them is gone, too."

"It's just their bodies here, not their souls," Mignon said.

"I think people want to be remembered. That's why they put up these gravestones, with their birth dates and their death dates."

We meandered along, stumbling over a sunken grave.

"Do you want to be remembered, Tommy?" she asked.

"Yeah, I guess so. After I'm gone, it'd be nice. But you got to do something real good or real bad to be remembered. I don't see that in my future."

"I don't think too much about the future when I'm gone," she said, looking at another old gravestone.

"Well, it's annoying to know that there's going to be a future where you won't be, just like there's a past where you never were."

She laughed and shook her head. Looking at her now, with the sun going down behind the bushes, I could only think of Madagascar and the slow dance. There was no future and no past when I was thinking about her.

"Maybe we should pray for these people," she said, out of the blue.

"Okay. You do it."

Mignon bowed her head and closed her eyes. "Dear God, we want to pray for all the people buried in this old cemetery. It doesn't seem that many people are remembering them, because they died a long time ago. We hope you remember them and take care of their precious souls. Amen."

She smiled. She seemed like a holy person to me. All she needed was a halo around her head. I'm exaggerating here, but not by much.

"Let's go before it gets dark," I said.

"Okay."

We could exit down the hill and take a short cut into a small park, where some women were playing with their kids. As we started picking our way through the fallen tombstones and metal markers, we saw a man with a big trash bag in his hand. He was a Double-A man with a short white beard and long thin arms. He was picking up trash and putting it in the bag.

"Hello," Mignon said.

"Howdy," he said back.

He picked up a brown beer bottle and put it in his sack. It clanked against other bottles.

"You're not back here to mess around, are you?" he asked.

"No, sir," I said. "Just going home."

"I didn't even know there was a cemetery back here," Mignon told him.

"Most people don't, but some kids come here at night and mess around. Smoke weed, drink beers, and throw their trash around. They have no respect for the souls here."

"We don't do that," Mignon said.

"She prayed for them, just a minute ago," I told him.

"Good. That's real good." He paused from his work and looked straight at us. "Do you know who's buried here?"

"No, sir."

"Well, this is an old Negro cemetery. You know, they wouldn't let black people be buried in the white folks' cemeteries back in the day. So this is where they came to rest. Half the people in here probably grew up in slavery, yes sir. Born into slavery and come out of it. So people should have a little respect, don't you think?"

"Yes, sir."

There was a roll of thunder overhead. We hadn't noticed the clouds moving in.

"Get on now. Head on home," he said with a big smile.

And we did, squirming through the brambles, past the crying babies in the park and out onto Glenwood. We started running to beat the rain. I was heading straight and Mignon had to turn.

"Thanks for taking me there," she said.

"My pleasure."

"See ya," she called out as she dashed home.

The first big drop hit me on the head and I sprinted.

I reached my door just before the heavy rain hit. I hoped Mignon made it, too. I was glad she had the heart to pray for those old souls.

CHAPTER ELEVEN

AFTER SEAN TOLD me how they blow up the ice wall on the river to announce that it's spring, I started wondering if there was any event that would tell me it's spring here. The first thing that came to mind was our dining room. We never really eat there except for Thanksgiving, or when we have people over, but during tax season, it's the forbidden zone. It's where Mom keeps her files and does all her tax work.

So when Mom had cleared out all the files from the floor and the table and all the white envelopes had been mailed. When the cold plastic tablecloth was removed and the embroidered one was back on the table. When the glass fruit bowl was back in its proper place between the two candle holders and we could walk in and out of the dining room anytime we wanted. That's when we knew it was really spring.

Every week something new was blooming: flowers, bushes, and trees. The air was softer and warmer. I could wear shorts and a t-shirt to school some days. The baseball team had a couple of rain outs, but the rain was really good for the growing plants. Everything smelled better, including people. Baby birds were learning to fly. Tadpoles were becoming frogs. The girls were wearing bright skirts or shorts with no leggings. Even the night sky had changed. You could still see the dippers but there were new stars in the constellations of Leo and Hercules. The North Star was always there, leading you like you were an ancient sailor.

■

For Easter we all piled into the Odyssey and went up to Greensboro for dinner with Aunt Mary Rose. Mom was driving and Dad was holding a big ham he'd bought out in the country somewhere. It had only been a few months since Uncle Aaron passed away, and Aunt Mary Rose was real happy to see us. The weather was great and almost warm, so the table had been set up on the stone patio. Lots of people besides us were there: Aunt Mary Rose's sister, Jesse, and her husband. That girl Mabel, from Charlotte. The preacher from the funeral. A good friend of Uncle Aaron's from the bank, with his wife and three kids. The oldest was a boy Ella's age. His name was Bart. He seemed real uncomfortable in his dress shirt and bow tie.

The women fixed the food in the kitchen while the men stood out on the patio. A few were drinking beer. My Dad and the preacher had iced tea. Billy was watching TV in the family room and I went to say hello. "How you doing?" I asked him.

"Okay."

"What you watching?"

"Some old movie: 'Easter Parade'."

"I've never seen it."

"It's good. It's happy. That guy who dances is in it. I forget his name. It'll come to me. He makes dancing look easy."

Take it from me, I thought, dancing is not easy, and I guess it's impossible for Billy. "Looks like a lot of people will be here today."

"Free food," he said. "Just kidding. I was hoping for more girls."

"Looking for a date?"

"You said it. I'd really like to get next to that Mabel. What a figure. But you can't do cousins."

I laughed. "Is it illegal?"

Billy laughed, too, and cut off the TV. It took him a minute but he got himself up from his chair. "I'm getting hungry," he said.

"Me, too."

Billy got his balance and wiped a hand across his hair, as if to put it in place. Then he looked straight at me with his grey eyes. "Tommy, let me tell you something. If your Daddy dies, it's a different world. Take my word for it."

I didn't want to think about that. We walked out to the patio. Billy's brother had arrived. He'd had his license for a couple of months. The car keys were swinging in his hand. His date was a girl name Felicity (I guess named after the TV show). She was loud and almost coming out of her dress. But Aaron Junior seemed to like her a lot. He'd hold her hand or give her a quick hug. She was probably nervous to meet all these strangers. I could understand that she was trying to be friendly, but her laugh was so strange, kind of like a donkey bray. Unfortunately she seemed to find a lot of things funny during dinner.

Anyway, the preacher got up to say grace and everybody paused.

"Heavenly father, we thank you for this bounty and this sweet weather and for this wonderful coming together of friends and family on this holiday of the resurrection. We come here still missing Aaron, our loved one, our friend, a father and a brother, a trusted coworker and a faithful Christian. But we are comforted by our faith, especially at Easter time: our heartfelt belief that this life is only the preamble for the eternal life of the soul. Amen."

There was a chorus of amens from the group. Felicity looked like she was wiping away a tear. I wondered what made her cry. Then we started some serious eating. Fried chicken and ham. There was a mountain of my favorite food: mashed potatoes. The gravy looked like lava running down the side of a volcano. I wondered, would you be able to eat this well in heaven, or would food be unnecessary? That would be a shame. Mom had made two really good pies, pecan and apple. They were gone in a minute. Ella spent some time chasing around with Bart in the yard. Aaron Junior stayed around long enough to say thank you to everybody for coming, and then he grabbed Felicity and headed for the door. As they walked by, her perfume almost knocked me over, it was so strong. It wasn't Madagascar, but more like the smell you get from those odor-fighting trees people hang from their car mirrors.

"Fred Astaire." Billy said to me when we got ready to leave.

"What?"

"That's the guy in 'Easter Parade'—the dancer. Fred Astaire." He seemed very pleased with himself. I gave him a fist bump.

On the way home, we went by the cemetery where Uncle Aaron was buried. We walked to the grave. The grass was just starting to grow, but the marker was already in the ground with his name and the day he was born and the day he died. Dad stood by the grave for a long time. Ella took some flowers from another grave and tried to put them on Uncle Aaron's.

"We don't do that, honey," Mom said and took Ella by the hand. "Now, show me where you got those."

While they were replacing the flowers, I was studying Dad, thinking about what Billy had said to me earlier. What if Dad was gone and in the grave? Things would not be right and might never be right again.

▪

I injured myself in the game against Wilson, when I slid into second and jammed my ankle. For a week I had to hobble around and miss practice and a game. I used the free time to watch Mignon play in her matches. As usual, she played great. She was graceful and could turn on a dime. Am I being too obvious? Am I pathetic?

Micky had a birthday party during my injury time

out and a bunch of us ended up at Game Land, playing some laser tag like we were nine again and racing around the go-kart track. After gaming we went to a Thai restaurant that Micky's uncle owns and had dinner with all this weird food. At first, Kareem didn't want to eat anything but after he tasted my noodles he got more adventurous. I had some chicken in a spicy yellow sauce. Kareem ordered shrimp with coconut on it. He loved it. David wanted to try everything (he's got an iron stomach) and so did Bobby Patel. Being Indian, he's used to spicy food.

It was a great party. It had been a long time since we'd all hung out together. Eight guys. We've known each other from elementary school days. It was fun getting together, but all the time I kept thinking about Mignon. I'm sure Kareem was thinking about Latitia. In the old days, a girl would have never crossed my mind when I was with my buds. Things, as Mr. Darwin said, evolve.

■

Now, at this point, I have to report a little on the home life. We'd been going to church more regularly since the Incident. For a change, Dad was with us every time, unless he had some kind of emergency at his shop. I didn't mind church so much. I had dropped Sunday School, but Ella was going from time to time. After each session, she'd relate a story from the Bible that she'd had trouble with, such as Jonah in the whale or Daniel in the lion's den. She thought the Noah voyage was a crock, and she said so to the teacher, Miss Fellows. Miss Fellows was understanding and tried to explain it as a story with a meaning but with some uncertain facts. "Like the movies," Ella had said.

The sermons Reverend Wallace gave followed different themes. One was that we were being judged by our actions and the other was that Jesus welcomes everybody, no matter their background or the sins of the past. So the judging part is tough and strict, but the Jesus part is about forgiveness and mercy as long as you have faith. But what about those millions of people who came before Jesus and had been doing their best to understand where they were and what the heck was the purpose of their lives? They'd been making beautiful things, like the jewelry and sculptures I saw at the museum one time. They'd fought in wars and made up tales. They invented bread and cheese. They named the stars and sailed the oceans. But they didn't have the faith of the Methodist church. Were they doomed?

When I talked to Mom about this one Sunday after dinner, here's what she said.

"I basically concentrate on the red letters in the Bible, to be honest. You know, the words that Jesus supposedly said. I don't read what other people say about the Bible. Everybody likes to mold things to fit what they think. Some people go to church, because it's like putting in an application for heaven. That's what they're interested in. I don't know about all that. When you get down to it, being a Christian is just 'do unto others as you would have them do unto you.' That's it, and 'Judge not, that you be not judged.' I think that's somewhere in Matthew. You want to help those who need it, and not look for a reward. It's not real complicated."

With that, she started picking up the dishes and I jumped up to help her. Jake was right behind me, looking for something that might fall from a plate.

"I just wish the music was better at church," I said.

"Well, you've got a point."

Of course, none of this answered my questions or my worries. I began to think that nobody had one answer, but that you had to keep searching.

Church was one way to search, and it had its attractions. I love singing hymns, but most of the Methodist ones are kind of dry. In fact most hymns have a sadness to them. The organ wails and the voices sadly answer.

I went to a Baptist church once. They sang "Onward Christian Soldiers," which made me feel weird like I was in the Crusades. But the best time I ever had singing in church was at a Double-A church downtown. I went there with our Sunday school group. Talk about music. They had an actual band playing and a big choir. A young girl with big rhinestone-decorated glasses played the drums. Everybody got into it. The whole church was filled with joy. I was a little shy when the service started, but after the first chorus of the first hymn, I was up on my feet and swaying like the others. Two old ladies, with enormous hats on their heads, were sitting in front of me. The hats were covered in feathers and flowers and ribbons. And the ladies held their hands up and shouted hallelujahs. And I shouted hallelujah. When I walked out of that service and into our van for the ride home, Hallelujah was still in my head.

■

Ella and Mom started a little garden in the backyard. They turned the soil over and added some sick-smelling compost. Dad and I made a kind of trellis for the beans to grow on. I wanted carrots, which I planted in a big clay pot. (They need deep soil.) We were growing beans, lima beans, and snap beans and a small patch of eggplant and some tomatoes. There was also some cucumber and red peppers. It looked pretty disorganized at first, but when you figured it out, it made sense. I have to say that Ella really worked at it. She even planted some herbs by herself in small pots: rosemary, mint, basil, and oregano. She tended them like they were her pets. She even talked to them when she thought we weren't paying attention. "Are you feeling okay? Are you thirsty?"

So things were growing. And Mignon and me were getting closer. We had our first "date"—I'd call it that, even though it wasn't supposed to be a date. She was going to the mall with Jeannie, and I said I might meet them there. I knew that I'd go, but I didn't want to seem too eager. Mom dropped me off and I found Mignon in the Apple store. We messed with the new iPads for a few minutes.

"Are you going to the movies?" I asked.

"We were." She gave me a funny look. I was confused.

"Jeannie can't come," Mignon said. "Her mom said she had to stay home. She just texted me. Some kind of punishment. Her mom's real strict."

So we were alone together in public, finally. Alone, of

course, with people swirling around.

"You still want to go to the movies?" I asked.

"I guess. Do you?"

"Depends on what's playing?"

That was a total lie. I would have gone to see anything with her. We had enough money for popcorn and one drink. The theater was more than half-empty. We sat towards the back. The movie was some kind of super-hero action thing. To be honest, I don't remember the name or what it was about. All I remember is feeling Mignon's hand on mine when things got tense, and then, when the monster leapt out at the hero, how she grabbed me and buried her face in my shoulder. Thank God for the digital surround-sound, which I hoped would cover the loud pounding of my heart.

"Sorry, it just freaked me out," she whispered.

"No problem."

"What happened?"

"The monster got zapped into a sizzling, disgusting jelly."

"Glad I missed it."

Back in the sunlight, we strolled around and did some people-watching. Mignon wanted to look at some cool shoes, so I went with her. She wanted to save some money and buy some new sandals for summer. We saw a few people from school. Brenda Banks and Liz Something-or-other were having some frozen yogurt. Suddenly I realized that I'd told Mom to pick me up at five, and it was five minutes till. Time had just sped by. Hours didn't seem like hours. Is that what the theory of relativity is about? I wasn't going to investigate that right then.

"Do you need a ride home?" I asked.

"I was going to call my Dad," she said, giving a look to her phone.

"You can go with us, unless you want to hang out some more."

"I'm ready to go."

On the way to the Odyssey, I realized that Mom had never met Mignon, and vice versa. And to add to the tension, Ella was staring out of the window, her runny nose pressed against the glass. She yelled "shotgun" as we approached, and jumped into the front seat next to Mom. The back door slid open.

"Mom, this is Mignon." I was jittery.

"Well, hello. Nice to finally meet you. I've heard so much about you."

All I could think was that too much information was possible.

"And this is my sister, Ella," I said pointing out the obvious.

"Hey, Ella."

"Hello," Ella said, squinting up at Mignon.

"Thought we could give Mignon a ride home."

"Sure thing," Mom said, and started the motor.

"What kind of name is Mignon?" Ella asked.

"Well, it's French," Mignon said.

"Never heard of it before except a filet....."

"Don't say it," I butted in. "You know how many time she's heard that?"

"You don't have to get so out of shape," Ella told me.

Mom changed the subject. "I hear you're a good soccer player." We were on the road now. Thank God.

"I'm okay."

"She's better than okay," I said.

"Ella loves soccer," Mom said.

"I wouldn't say I love it," Ella corrected her.

"I mean, you really like playing."

"Sometimes," Ella declared. "When I'm in the mood."

"And Mignon, I hear that you like to dance." Mom wouldn't stop. Mignon gave me a nudge. Oh, God. It was going to be as I had feared.

"Yes, I do." Mignon glanced at me and I made a face. I don't know what that face might have looked like, but it must have been painful to see.

"So do I," Mom said. "But it's so hard to get good partners."

Mignon nodded. "You can say that again."

Could I jump out of the car at the stoplight? I tried to cut off the conversation, but they were jabbering at top speed. They talked about school and grades and where Mignon grew up and what her father did (biotech, I think) and did they eat much Cajun food. Ella just zoned out on her DS. Why was I so nervous? When we finally stopped to let Mignon out in front of her house and they said "nice to meet you," I took my first deep breath.

"She's so talky," Ella said.

"She seems very nice, Thomas. A mother can tell. You should have her come over for dinner one night."

I couldn't think of anything more stress-creating. "That's a good idea," I lied.

"Not," Ella said.

That night, Mignon FaceTimed me. She was in her pajamas. "I like your sister," she said. "She's cute and funny."

"Yeah, and she knows it too."

She laughed. "You think?"

"Do you ever wish you had a sister or a brother?" I asked.

"Sometimes."

"It's good, but every now and then it can be a pain in the butt."

"Yeah. I was supposed to have a sister, but mom had a miscarriage. She lost the baby."

"That's too bad." I didn't know what a miscarriage actually was, but I got the idea.

"I was just two years old when it happened, so I don't remember anything about it. I guess it was bad, because they didn't try to have another baby."

"Did your parents talk to you about it?" I asked.

"No. The only thing I know is that they were going to name her Catherine."

"Nice name," I said.

"Yeah, Catherine Alice Eubanks. Pretty, isn't it?"

"Yeah."

"She'd be about the same age as Ella if she'd lived." There was a long pause. "Well, good night," she said.

"See you later," I said. The screen went dead.

Who was this Catherine? What was she? Was she a small soul? Was she a snowflake or a star? Or was she nothing at all, just something remembered?

▪

When my injury healed and I started playing baseball again, I had one hero moment that I really enjoyed. I scored the winning run in a game against our so-called arch-rival, Otis.

It was a three/three tie, and I managed a luckout single to right field. (I could hear my Dad saying, "You're late" in the batting cage, and I was, but it fell in.) With one out, Solano bunted me to second. Now there were two outs in the last inning and the yankee, Sean, was up. He missed the first pitch, waving at it as if he was blind. The next one was too high. But he hit the third pitch into left field. It was a screamer. Like I say, I'm not the fastest player, so I wasn't sure I could make it home. Coach Wrenn was waving me on, but there was doubt on his puffy face. I chugged as fast as I could. Benson signaled to me to get down, but I didn't want to rehurt my ankle, so I didn't make a normal slide.

I went in head first. I actually slid past the plate, but I managed to touch it as I went by in a cloud of red dust. We won! Everybody starting yelling and piling on. I felt pretty good, especially since Mignon was in the bleachers with Jeannie and Ramona Schenk. In my brief athletic career, that might have been the high point. At Andy's Pizza after the game, the team gave me a game ball, which they all signed, and I took a big bow.

▪

This spring a lot of things were happening. Dad finally

finished the Norton, and one Sunday afternoon after church, he rolled the bike out of the garage and into the driveway. All the chrome had been polished up and the paint looked fresh and bright. Mom even came out to take a look. Jake studied us from the steps, his nose twitching.

"It's real pretty, Rick," Mom said. "Looks great."

Dad nodded, just like his old self. Then he straddled the bike and kicked it to life. The engine caught and sputtered and then roared as he turned the throttle. Jake charged down the step, barking and jumping at the metal beast. Dad let the engine warm up into a steady sound. "Wanna go for a ride?" he asked Mom. She shook her head.

"Tommy?" Dad asked.

I looked at Mom and she didn't say no.

"You've got to wear helmets," she ordered.

I ran into the garage and got the two helmets. Mom looked nervous. Ella finally came out of the house, still holding her DS. "What's all the noise?" she shouted.

And then we are off, past the park and on to Glenwood. Traffic was picking up with people heading to the malls or going home after Sunday lunch. Dad got the bike going pretty good when we found a stretch of semi-country road. I say semi, because you could still see pieces of farms every now and then. An old barn would be sitting in a field, but it would be next to a bunch of apartments that were being built.

The two-lane road was pretty straight, so Dad made a

turn onto another road that led up a small hill, and we were suddenly in real country with slow turns and what I call ups and downs. I held on tight as we streaked along. I couldn't help thinking about Uncle Aaron, and I wondered if Dad was thinking about him, too. Finally, Dad pulled off the road and turned to me. The bike was idling and popping.

"These old bikes are really raw. But she runs pretty good, don't you think?"

I gave him a thumbs-up. "Sweet."

"Let's go back home before your mother has a heart attack."

He turned the bike around and we streaked through some other ups and downs, took a couple more fast turns, and then we were in traffic again. A guy leaned out of his Ram truck and asked Dad if he wanted to sell the Norton.

"For the right price. I'm putting it on eBay and Craig's list tomorrow."

The man nodded and we kept moving.

When we pulled into the driveway, Mom was still there, arms folded like she hadn't moved in all that time. Jake came running up barking and snarling again until Dad cut the engine and rolled the Norton back in the garage.

"That was fun," I said to Mom, but she didn't comment.

▪

Dad listed the Norton the next day, and sure enough, that same Ram truck appeared in our driveway. The man's name was Harvey Norton, as it turned out. I don't know if he liked the bike or just the name. He paid Dad a lot of money in cash and rolled the bike up a ramp and into the truck. His son, who was about 15, helped tie the bike down in the bed. I asked if the bike was for him. "No way," he said, with a sad shake of the head. Then, in a minute after the handshake, the Norton was gone. Dad watched the truck disappear down the street. Mom came out to say dinner was ready. She looked pretty happy. Dad looked like he'd lost a friend.

The next weekend, Dad was picking up his tools and storing them in the garage. I helped a little, but there wasn't much talking, aside from "Hand me that wrench." After the garage was organized and cleaned up, it was neat but sad. Dad even got the oil stains up.

I couldn't remember a time when the Norton wasn't sitting there. I liked watching Dad work on it. He'd be in a fog, concentrating on figuring out a problem. So for a while after the Norton was sold, everybody but Ella got real quiet at dinner. Mom would try to make small talk, but Dad's mind was somewhere else.

Then one afternoon, Dad was late coming home from work. When he pulled up, he was towing an old car. It was a dark (maybe blue) convertible that said Fiat on the wheel hubs. The car was pretty dirty and had a dent in the driver's door. But the interior looked like it was red leather. Was this like the Italian car that he had worked on with his Dad?

"What do you think, sport?" Dad asked me.

"It's cool. Really cool."

"It's gonna need a lotta work. I'll need your help."

"Sure thing." That could be fun, I thought.

Mom came out. "Where'd you dig that up?" Mom asked.

"It sort of found me," Dad said with a wink.

"What is it?"

"It's an Italian thing."

"Italian? I hope you didn't pay too much for it," Mom said.

"I'm not telling."

"It'll keep you out of trouble, I guess."

"Maybe."

She smiled and shook her head. Me and Dad pushed the Fiat into the clean garage. The tires were almost flat and the windshield had a chip. But it was a beauty. Once we got the car inside Dad looked it over one more time, checked a rip in the top, and then looked at me. "What's for dinner?" he asked.

"It's appropriate." I said. "Pizza."

He laughed the biggest laugh I'd heard from him in a long time. He pushed me towards the door just as Ella poked her head out. "Is that what you call a sporty car?" she asked.

"Yep," I said.

"Snazzy." She ducked back into the house. Where'd she hear that word? Maybe on "Sponge Bob" or "Glee"?

CHAPTER TWELVE

ALL MY CRAZY thoughts about the universe and life on Earth would come and go. I kind of looked at it like a tropical disease. You know, you can get malaria and they treat you and you feel fine. Months go by and all of a sudden the symptoms pop up again. It doesn't kill you, but you're never free of the disease. You just keep treating the symptoms.

It's the stars that kick in my disease and they're always there. Even when I'm not at the park or down at the beach with the star map, I just have to look up at night. I've gotten good at identifying certain constellations. And if I see something in the paper or magazine or on TV about galaxies and nebulae and black holes, I get into it. I start trying to think in light years, which is impossible to do. It still makes me a little queasy, but I can't resist. And then there were new things that added to my pile of thoughts. Mainly that your life, your ordinary life, could go away in a flash of bad luck.

One night after I'd finished my homework and had

some FaceTime with Mignon, I turned the TV on to the Discovery channel. I started watching a show about this mummy, the Iceman (they called him Otzi) who was discovered frozen in the Alps, in 1991. He'd been frozen up there for thousands of years and then some ice melted and his head came sticking out into the sunshine. (Did the melting come from global warming? They didn't say.) Otzi's mummy body was pretty intact. Scientists figured the Iceman was a hunter. Had he gotten lost or had he been tracking some kind of animal and been caught in a blizzard? He had a copper ax and a bow and arrows. He had a knife and a flint for making fire, and he was wearing waterproof shoes. Or so they said. He had strange tattoos that nobody could figure out.

Well, anyway, they'd been studying this guy for more than 20 years. First they dated him. He was about 4,000 years old. They even were able to figure out what he'd been eating—an animal called an ibex, which is like a mountain goat, and some bread. They studied his DNA. They used all kinds of new scientific equipment to inspect him. At first, they thought he'd just frozen to death. But then they found wounds on him and were able to tell that he'd been hit very hard in the head. So he was probably murdered. It was amazing what they could figure out.

Anyway, the point of telling you this is that after all that study, with all these special instruments and the smartest people in their fields, they knew a lot about Otzi and even how he died, but they still didn't really know him. What did he like to do? Did he sing or dance? What did he think about the stars? Did he worship the moon or the sun or something else? Did he have a girlfriend or a favorite tune? So even though they could figure out so many things about him, they didn't know who he really was. That just set me thinking even more about myself and whether anybody would ever know or care who I was. That was the question. Did it matter? It seemed to matter to me.

▪

I mentioned Otzi to a few people, and I think most of them thought I was a little nutty. Mignon was the only one who sort of got it. She was sitting by the fountain at the mall. (We called it The Fountain of the Dancing Dorks. You'd have to see it to understand the name. The sculpture consisted of five bronze boys jumping in the water, but their faces look old and crazy.) I had just dodged a Cadillac as I jogged over to her from the mall parking lot where Mom had dropped me off.

"Picture this," I said. "I'm waiting to cross the street, and a crazed teenager loses control of his daddy's Escalade while texting and mows me down. I'm dead and I'm 12."

"That would suck," Mignon said, playing with the necklace I'd given her.

"For whatever reason, the chance that I could just be gone and nobody ever know I was here or who I was bothers me."

"That's just the way it is," she said. "Think of all those people who built the pyramids for the Pharaohs. They died and who knows where they're buried. The Pharaoh and his family are inside the pyramid with all their favorite stuff."

"I got stuff," I said without thinking.

"Well, maybe you should build yourself a pyramid."

We started walking in the mall, just wandering. I was imagining the pyramids.

"Let's get a pretzel," she said.

We walked up to the food court and bought a couple. Mignon stopped for a moment, pausing between bites. She was thinking—standing still as if frozen. And then she spoke. "You could make a time capsule?"

"What?"

"A time capsule. It's simple. I remember when we were back in Louisiana, we went to a ceremony at a new church. The church had just been built and they put together a time capsule for the day they were blessing the new church. It was a metal box that they sealed in the wall. It was to be opened when they would celebrate the church's 100-year anniversary."

"What was in it?"

"Stuff from that date—newspapers and church bulletins. I don't know exactly."

"Was it big?"

"No. Just a box thing." She took the last bite of her pretzel. "Then, if a meteor hits you in the head or a stoned teenager runs over you or you choke to death on some of the country-fried steak at lunch, well, there'll be a record of you and some of the stuff you liked for somebody to find." She was kidding, I think.

Some ideas just click with you when you hear them.

Your mind kind of holds them for a minute, inspects them, and then the thought explodes and you get excited. It's like all the parts of your brain get in sync. The idea seemed perfect. "I think you're a genius," I said.

"Thanks." She had a funny look on her face.

"I'm serious."

"Are we going to the movies? Jeannie's coming and I think that MacDonald guy is coming with Brenda."

"No. I've got planning to do." My mind was whirling.

"Planning what?" she asked.

"What you just said."

"So you can't go to the movies?" She was disappointed.

"I wouldn't be able to concentrate," I told her. She looked annoyed. "It's your idea," I reminded her.

"Like I've said before, you get too worked up. It's just an idea."

"But maybe it's the right idea," I said. I was churning.

She must have seen a wild look in my eyes, because she shrugged. "So, what are you waiting for? Get it out of your system. Go."

And I went.

▪

A time capsule. Something that could be discovered a long time from today. That night I sat at my little desk, which dated back to fifth grade. Dr. Bugg had made if for Dad. It was a trade. Dad tuned Dr. Bugg's Subaru in exchange. I tried making a list of things that could go into the time capsule. The first version was so long I'd need a storage unit to pack in all the stuff I was thinking about. I'd included my bike and my beat-up sled. How about sports equipment? Gloves. Bats. Old sweatbands.

I texted a copy of my list to Mignon. She texted back, "hahahaha too big." I had to calm down and think more about what I really liked and what I could include in this time capsule. It was going to be harder than I thought. Maybe it wasn't a perfect idea.

What did I like to eat? That was important for folks in the future to know. Mom's lasagna for number one. Barbecue and hush puppies. I liked pizza. Pot roast in the winter. My favorite dessert had to be banana pudding or Ben and Jerry's Chocolate Fudge Brownie ice cream. Mom made great oatmeal cookies. I did like pecan pie and rice pudding, too, but only every now and then. How about Thanksgiving dinner? Turkey and all the stuff that went with it aside from the Brussels sprouts.

I went to Mom.

"Mom, could you write down your recipe for lasagna?"

"Really?"

"Yeah."

"What are you gonna do with it?" she asked.

"It's part of a project."

"Okay, but I kind of do it from memory, and feel. I taste it, and add a little of this or that."

"Just write it down as best you can."

"Okay. You're so serious."

"Could you do it soon? It's kind of a deadline thing," I said, sprinting back to my room.

■

Mignon finally came to dinner and it wasn't lasagna. Dad broke out the grill and went deep and got some filet mignons in her honor from the Meat Shack. Mom made some double-baked potatoes and asparagus. Green beans, optional for my sister. As usual, the discussion of Mignon's name came up.

"What exactly does it mean?" Dad asked as he brought in the steaks.

"Dad, people ask her that all the time," Ella butted in. "It's French. It means 'cute' or 'sweet' or something like that."

"Thanks," Dad said.

"It's a nice name," Mom put in.

"I know it's strange, but I'm okay with it."

We all ate the steaks. Even Ella. They were delicious. Dad talked about the Fiat. Mom talked about how happy she was that tax season was over. Mignon talked about running track next year, because she just likes running. I didn't say much at all.

"What's your favorite subject?" Mom asked Mignon.

"Art, I guess."

"She's a really good artist." I had to say something. Those swans on the moonlit lake were in my mind.

"I like art, too," Ella said.

And that's how it went for about 35 minutes. After we wolfed down the pie—"pie á la mode" Mom called it, because of the ice cream—we excused ourselves to my cave of a room. We hadn't mentioned the time capsule at all but we were thinking about it.

"You shouldn't tell anybody," Mignon said, sitting on

my bed.

"Not even Micky?"

"Especially not Micky. He's nosy and he's a gossip."

▪

Micky is all that. Last week he was desperate to get a girl-friend for the summer. His parents rent a place down at Surf City every July for two weeks. He was hoping that some girls would be around. Last summer a couple of cute girls from Canada were staying two doors down. Even though they were fourteen he tried to make contact, but, after they told a couple of lame Asian jokes, he realized they were racists. Of course, he was willing to overlook that if he could get some "action". He never explained what action he meant. In any case he wasn't successful. While he was explaining this incident to me, he started talking about girls in general. "I'd hate to be a girl," he said.

"Why?"

"So much drama. And the monthly bleeding. What's up with that?"

The very idea froze me. "I wouldn't like it."

"You know, there are tribes in Africa or Polynesia somewhere, when the women have their periods, they put 'em away in a hut."

"That's kind of awful. Where'd you hear that?" I asked.

"I don't remember. My parents take National Geographic."

"Maybe that happened a long time ago," I said.

"That's not as bad as if they were in Kuwait or

somewhere, all covered up in that hot weather and then have to bleed. Geez." It was obvious that this was a subject that fascinated him.

"Somehow they get used to it, I guess."

"My brother, Duncan, he says they get real bitchy and cranky when they're bleeding. Something to do with hormones. So you never know. You might just say hello and if they're in that bitchy time, they'll just cut you down."

First, let me say that Duncan is an odd name for a boy of 18 whose parents are both Thai. Micky explained it this way. There was a man named Duncan who helped his parents when they first moved here. He took a real interest in them. Turns out he'd been in Vietnam during the war there and had spent time in Thailand, too. His parents thought he might have been CIA. Anyway they liked this man so much that they named their first, American-born, son after him. Duncan became a very good violinist and gave concerts when he was eight or nine. He's in college now and doesn't play the violin anymore.

"Does Mignon have her period? That's what they call it…The Period. Has she started?" Micky asked.

"I don't know. What kind of question is that?"

"She never gets bitchy?"

"Not really."

"You could ask her?" He wouldn't stop.

"No, I couldn't. I don't want to."

"It's a natural thing. It may have something to do with the moon and the tides. That should interest you."

"Let me suggest something. When you go to the beach this summer, why don't you start asking the girls you meet about this? That should be an icebreaker."

Micky started laughing and gave me a high five and a final fist bump.

■

Back to the dinner night. Mignon and I sitting in my room. For starters, I couldn't believe that she was in my room. She was coiled on my bed. Ella strolled past but didn't stop.

"I have to put music in there," I said.

"Absolutely," she said.

"But you know how many songs I've got on my phone?"

"Same here. But you have to decide on the really important ones."

"You're right. I'll put the important ones on a CD or flash drive. But who knows whether in a thousand years or so they'll know how our digital stuff works."

"Maybe, but you have to chance it. Somehow people figured out those hieroglyphics in Egypt," she reminded me.

"Well, people in the future will be very advanced— brainiacs, maybe."

"Or a bunch of desperate tribes or something—like in the movies, when aliens are destroying the world."

"According to Mr. Henkel, we're doing a pretty good job of that ourselves."

"Anyway, you can't predict the future like that." She looked over her music list on her phone. "What do you like now? American Authors?"

"Not really. One song maybe. I like the Granules' new

album. I like the Lumineers."

"'Stubborn Love'?" she asked.

"Yeah, and that song, 'Dead Sea'," I added.

"I like that one, too."

"What really sticks?" I asked myself out loud.

I got my phone and looked through the songs. I gave Mignon the earbuds and played a classic—"Imagine," by John Lennon. She nodded and sang along softly. I watched her as she rocked side to side, sitting on my bed. Her eyes were closed; her lashes were long against her cheeks. Outside my window a half-moon hung in the tops of the pines. Could there be a better moment?

The song ended and she stood up. "I've got to go home."

"Too bad."

"Tommy, you just have to separate things and find what's important. What songs really mean something to you? I guess that applies to everything you're gonna put in there."

She was right. This time capsule thing was going to take some work and some real thinking. I walked her home that night. She said she was worried about a test she had on Monday. But something more than the test was on her mind. She wasn't being playful on the walk. No joking. No looks.

"Is something bothering you?" I asked.

"There's always something. Look at you with your stars and your obituaries."

"They're hobbies."

"You wish."

She smiled at me at last. We raced up the road to her house. I stopped on the sidewalk.

"I'm not walking you to the door. Pierre might be hiding somewhere and ambush me. I'm not in the mood for that."

"Chicken."

With that she looked around, as if to see if anybody was watching us, and then she kissed me on the cheek. Did she seem sad or was I imagining things again?

"Goodnight," she said. She jogged to her front door. "Don't Face-Time me tonight. I got to study."

"Me, too," I lied.

I walked back as slow as I could. The air was filled with honeysuckle from the edge of the park. I could still feel her kiss on my cheek, two blocks later. When I reached my house, Dad was in the garage and the Fiat's hood was up. Mom was cleaning the kitchen. Ella was probably glued to the TV.

"I'm back!" I shouted when I came through the door.

Ella popped out from the pantry. "Do you guys kiss?" she asked.

"What?"

"You heard me."

"None of your business. Piss off."

"Mom, Tommy told me to piss off!"

Now Mom appeared. "Did you say that?"

I wanted to bop Ella on the head. "Yeah. I'm sorry."

"I just asked him if they kiss. Big deal."

"It's none of your business, Ella," Mom said.

"That's what I meant."

"He doesn't have to say anything. I know they do." Ella wasn't giving up.

"Go to bed. Study. Something," Mom said.

With that, Ella, satisfied that she'd caused a commotion, darted up the stairs to her room. Mom looked at me and shook her head.

"What?" I asked.

"I'm not going to say it," Mom said.

"Say what?"

"That I like Mignon. Because if I do, you might go opposite and ruin a good thing."

"Everybody's into my business."

"See."

The kiss had just about faded from my cheek as I headed to my room and the task ahead.

CHAPTER THIRTEEN

ET ME BREAK in here and say something about school. I haven't written much about it, because other things seem to need more explanation. But school is important. For kids, it's like our job—our work every day except weekends and holidays. And even with the breaks, you might have to work on a project or study for a big test.

I want to make good grades and learn new stuff. But school is also social. I see my friends there. Some I haven't mentioned in this story yet. Jacob Meyer, for one. We have a lot of fun together in health class. He's great at telling jokes. He acts in school plays and he's always trying to get me to try out for one. Maybe next year. And there's Heather Bing and Justin Taylor and Brad Jenkins. If I had a birthday party, I'd have to invite at least fifteen people—maybe more. But the truth is, I don't see those people much after school. Unless people live in the same neighborhood we don't get together except for parties and school events. So how we get together really is on our phones and computers—Facebook or Twitter or Instagram. If I have a lot to say, I can email. We send photos when we're somewhere interesting or doing something crazy. I have a whole big relationship with Jacob Meyer just from Instagram. That's social networking for real.

The school building itself is a second home for all of us. The halls, the rooms, the bathrooms, the lunch room. We've been there several years and know how to find things and avoid things. Certain toilets don't flush too good. Some chairs in the lunch room you don't want to sit in. Etcetera. It's a comfort zone. Most of us try to pay attention to the teachers, because some subjects are hard to understand. Most of the teachers are okay. Miss Sanchez, the Spanish teacher, is a pain in the butt. Someone stole her sense of humor. How can you be a teacher if you don't have a sense of humor?

There are days when we get a little too rowdy or giddy. One day I started laughing at Jacob Meyer. It was nothing, really—just a funny accent he put on. I thought I was going to pee in my pants. Then Jacob laughed at me laughing. The teacher sent us to detention to calm down. But we couldn't stop, so finally they had to separate us. By lunch time we were sort of okay, but I couldn't look at him the rest of the day, because if I did it would start all over again. To this day, if Jacob says one word in that accent, I burst out laughing. What's that called? Laughophilia?

Some days you'd like not to go to school. If there's a big test that you're nervous about or you did something embarrassing the day before, you'd like to stay cuddled up under the covers and claim to be sick. But when you're really sick with a cold or a bad stomach and have to miss school, you miss it. You want to be there and you spend all night texting people to find out what happened in your absence. Does that qualify as what they call irony?

∎

Now, back to the music decisions. After I walked Mignon home, I spent part of the night listening to songs. How could I choose just a few? But you don't want too many. A lot of the songs I liked now would bore me in three or four weeks. I had to find ones with lasting power. Tunes that hung in your brain. The Granules, of course, both the first album and the second. Can't forget the Dips. Some old ones hung on, like "Dani California," by the Red Hot Chili Peppers. And then some classic songs by the Beatles and Rolling Stones.

There were tunes that were stuck in my head but I didn't know what they were called. One I remembered was from a concert at the symphony. We went as a class last year. It was classical music. I'm not into that kind of music, mainly because the pieces are so long and serious. But this one I remember, and curiously, sometimes when I'm out for a long ride on my bike, it pops in my head. At the concert a man played the main theme on a clarinet or maybe it was an oboe. That's the part I remember. It made me think that maybe there was other classical music I'd like. That's important. But what was it called? I thought Jacob Meyer might remember, because he was at the concert and he takes piano.

My knowledge of music is pretty poor. I've been trying to teach myself guitar for a couple of years. I do okay, but I'm not ready to play in public. I don't practice enough. But I did write a song. It's called "Leave me Alone." I wrote it for my sister, Ella, because she's always coming into my room without knocking or anything. She stands there, not saying anything, and stares at me until I chase her out. The theme of the song is asking people to leave me alone, but at the end of the song the singer realizes that he doesn't want to be lonely. Something like that. It's not finished.

Anyway, I finally fell asleep with my headphones on. The last song I remember hearing was the Beatles' "All You Need is Love."

The next day at school, I asked Jacob Meyer if he could remember the song from the concert. I hummed it.

"Rhapsody in Blue,' by George Gershwin. He's Jewish," he said. Whenever a famous person comes up who's Jewish, Jacob lets you know. It was a joke between us. He even claimed that Abraham Lincoln was Jewish because of his first name. As I understand it, Jews don't believe too much in the New Testament, and they aren't supposed to eat pork. But Jacob loves pork barbecue. "I'm a southern Jew," he said. "Those dietary laws are suspended down here. Otherwise, you'd starve to death."

So it was "Rhapsody in Blue". He said he'd trade me his copy of that for my Granules second album. It was a deal.

At lunch, Mignon wanted to know how things were

going. "Did you figure out which songs to put in there?"

"Not totally. It's hard. You can't put everything in. You're just choosing for this day, this week. That's it."

She nodded. "That's true about everything, isn't it? You don't know about the future and the past is gone. It's all about now, about this moment. You could think a lot different in a year or two." Then she picked up her tray and left. That was some deep thinking on her part. Was she thinking about us?

▪

The next day I found a cardboard box in the garage—the one our new toaster came in. It wasn't too large or too small. You didn't want something really big, because you'd have to carry it before you buried it. Too small and you couldn't put much in it, and finding it later on would be harder. So I put this box in my room and it became the Time Box. Capsule didn't describe what I was doing.

After music I wanted to put in books and other things. There was *Chinga, Unleashed,* a graphic novel I really liked. There was also my old copy of *Alice's Adventures in Wonderland* and *Through the Looking Glass.* I really like those books. "Beware the Jabberwock, my son/ The jaws that bite, the claws that catch!/ Beware the Jubjub bird, and shun/ the frumious Bandersnatch!" That's one of my favorite poems. Sometimes I use "frumious" to describe something powerful and awesome—like, "your new bike is frumious." Unless you know the books, you don't get it.

I had to include *To Kill a Mockingbird,* which we read this year. And the Bible; that's real important. And

Treasure Island. What a great book. Can't forget all the books by Lemony Snicket. Some books we read in school this past year were ho hums. One was about an Indian boy's life on a reservation and another one was about a girl who wanted to be an astronaut. I think that was a true story. All in all, just like with the music, things were stacking up and there were too many choices.

Mignon would come over some days after school or we'd meet in the park and I'd discuss what was on my mind. She didn't suggest anything specific, because she didn't want to interfere with my decisions. She wanted everything in the Time Box to be chosen totally by me, or at least that's what she said.

Because we were getting close to the end of school, we had other things to think and talk about. There were tests and papers on the horizon and, of course, friendship issues. She had a little problem with Jeannie, who'd invited her to the mountains in the summer. Jeannie's family had a house on a big lake outside of Asheville somewhere. In August they would go up there to escape the big heat down here. Jeannie wanted Mignon to come for a week or two, but Mignon said she couldn't and Jeannie was sulking.

"She's really peeved," Mignon said. "I told her I'm sorry, but I don't control things in my life."

"Couldn't you go for a few days or something?"

"No. Not in August."

"She'll get over it. You know that."

"Yeah, but she's been so bitchy the last few days. It's annoying. She's too attached to me."

"Could be. Yeah, I can see that."

"It's not healthy," she said.

Was she thinking of me too? "I just want to get my box finished," I said, changing the conversation.

"You're not going to use that cardboard thing, are you? It wouldn't last a month."

"Of course not. I've been thinking about what to use. I'll have to build something."

Mignon looked out my window, thinking. "It should probably be steel," she said.

"Too heavy. More like plastic. Remember Mr. Henkel said that plastic can be here almost forever if it's not in the sunlight or in acidy water."

"Yeah. That would be good."

"But first I've got to finish choosing what to put in the box."

"I have to go study," she said. She stood up, stretching her arms over her head. I loved watching her move now that the weather was good and she wasn't wrapped up in a big sweater or a puffy jacket. This day she was wearing a soft white dress with little flowers on it. The flowers were red like roses and purple like irises. When she moved, it seemed to move with her like it was part of her. She was wearing sandals and she had painted her toe nails—red on her right foot and purple on her left.

"Matching my dress, kind of," she said when she noticed me eyeing her toes. I was thinking that by next year we'd be really tight. Girlfriend and boyfriend, I hoped, but I'd have to ask for that, which was something I didn't know if I was prepared to do. I was glad she wasn't going to spend August with Jeannie in the mountains. We could work it out over the summer.

▪

So books were the first things I put into the box, starting with *To Kill a Mockingbird*. It was a paperback with some drawings I'd made inside the cover. Then my small Bible, which had been given to me by my Sunday school when I was in fourth grade. You could put it in your pocket. Then *Alice in Wonderland*—I thought twice about giving up my good, hardbound copy of that. The last book in— the Chinga book—was the heaviest. For good measure, I decided to copy a poem I liked from my English textbook: "Remember," by Christina Rossetti. Here are the last lines:

> Yet if you should forget me for a while
> And afterwards remember, do not grieve:
> For if the darkness and corruption leave
> A vestige of the thoughts that once I had,
> Better by far you should forget and smile
> Than that you should remember and be sad.

Next was the music. I made a CD with "Rhapsody in Blue", "Imagine" and "All You Need is Love." (I can't remember when I didn't know "Imagine.") I had to include three by the Granules—my favorite of those is "Happy and Lucky". One funny song by the Dips. I picked two from the Avett Brothers. (They're from around here.) Then "One and Only" by Adele, because I listened to it with Mignon once and she said how much she liked

Adele and that particular song. I made a note of that on the cover of the CD, but the truth is I'd started liking it a lot myself. (I'm listening to it now.) When I finished, I realized that there were 25 songs on the CD. A mix of old and new. I could have added 25 more songs, easy. It was tough to keep some out but you have to stop somewhere. When I was chasing down the Granules on the internet (they're kind of obscure), I ran into another group called La Granules, from France. Their music is really strange and they use weird instruments. It's hard to describe the sound, but it's pretty good. Worth a listen, but don't have a headache when you do.

Now, you can put all these things in a box, but you have to explain a little about why they're there. You have to imagine somebody digging up this box a thousand years from now and trying to figure out what's what.

"Maybe you should record something explaining the books and the music," Mignon suggested.

We were in the park, as usual, and Mignon was stretched out on a picnic table. Johnny Shelton was by the basketball court, smoking and waiting for somebody. The rumor was that if you wanted some weed, he was the guy to talk to. The dogwoods were finally in full bloom and the air was filled with sweet smells.

"I don't know," I said. "I worried about the Bible. Will people understand that a thousand years or more from now?"

"Why not?"

"Well, it's religious. Maybe in a thousand years, there won't be Christianity."

"It's lasted more than two thousand years so far." Mignon advised me.

"Maybe it will be more than a thousand years before somebody finds the box. Maybe it will be five thousand years. Who knows?"

"So?"she asked.

"So I wrote a little thing about Christianity and put it in the Bible," I said in my defense.

"What did you say?"

"I said if you boiled it down to the basics, it's about being good to your fellow man. It's about not being selfish."

"How about heaven?"

"I covered that by saying that if you read the book and believe in Jesus, you're promised everlasting life in a place called heaven."

Mignon sat up and looked around. Another guy was with Johnny Shelton now and they were laughing and smoking.

"Isn't this kind of heaven?" she said. "I mean, the way the light is in the trees and all the blooms, the birds singing, and that warm breeze coming across the creek."

She smiled at me and seemed to be waiting for me to answer. I just nodded, because I couldn't say anything. Yes, the dogwood blooms and the gold light in the trees and the smell of the honeysuckle were all part of it. But for me, this was heaven because Mignon was there, sitting on the picnic table, and she was my best friend. I'd never had a girl be my best friend. How had that happened? All I knew was that I was happy with her nearby. I was happy when she gave my sleeve a tug. I was happy when she laughed at my jokes or pushed my hair from my eyes or talked about heaven.

"I made an A on the English test," she said, breaking my dreaminess.

"Great."

"Let's go home. I need to study for my government test." We headed towards our bikes. "What did you make?" she asked.

"Got a B."

She looked at me suspiciously. "Liar."

"Why do you say that?"

"Cross your heart?"

I stopped, but I didn't cross my heart. "Why does it matter what I made?"

"I have to beat you once on a test or project. Once."

"You got your wish. I got an A-minus."

"Yay!" she jumped up and spun around in the air. When she stopped spinning, she got in my face. "You better not be lying."

"Or what?"

She swung at me, a big roundhouse swing that I dodged. She started to swing again and I rushed her, tackling her into a forsythia bush. We lay for a minute in the yellow flowers, still caught in each other's arms, laughing.

"Liar," she said again.

Heaven, yes indeed.

CHAPTER FOURTEEN

BASEBALL SEASON ENDED when we, the brave Argonauts, were eliminated from the conference tournament by the Dillard Devils, four to one. I played okay, which means I didn't make any big errors. I got one hit but was wiped out on a double-play.

After the game, which was on our home field, Kareem, Micky, and I sat around and goofed. "Take my picture," I said, and handed Micky my phone. I posed next to the backstop fence. I was wearing my uniform, still covered with red dust from my slide into second.

"Hold a bat. That looks cool," Micky said.

"Big league," Kareem added.

I leaned on a bat like I was on deck. My glove was at my feet.

"Got it," Micky said, and handed back the phone.

"Now, you two. Stand up. I want to take your picture."

They were sitting on the old bleachers. When they stood up, Kareem was more than a head taller than Micky. He put his elbow on top of Micky's spikey hair. I took the picture; studied it. It looked good.

"Why all the picture-taking?" Kareem asked.

"I'm doing a project."

"What kind of project?"

"Can't tell you." No way could I tell them about the Time Box.

"You can't tell us—your buds?" Micky asked.

"No, I can't. Maybe later."

"You're getting weird, man." Kareem picked up the bat and took some air swings.

"Yes, he is," Micky agreed. "Since he got so tight with Mignon, we don't see him as much. And now he's got secret projects."

"He's got coochie on the brain." Kareem said, cocking the bat.

I pitched him a mud clod which he smashed into a hundred piece with his big swing.

"What are you guys doing for the summer? Camp or something?" Micky asked.

"I'm going to basketball camp in Chapel Hill," Kareem said. "That's first, and then there's another one at Wake Forest. That one's a real camp. I sleep there. It kind of eats up the summer."

School was really winding down. Did summer always have to be so filled up with stuff?

"I'm not doing anything. Just hanging around," I said. "I'll help my dad with this old car he wants to restore. Then we may go to the beach for a week, in July or August."

"So you're saying you'll be around?" Micky asked.

"Sort of. You?"

"Well, I have to visit my aunt and uncle in Maine for a week, right after school."

"What's Maine like?" I asked.

"It's pretty, but the water's real cold. I don't get much swimming in. Mostly we eat lobster. But then I come back and head for the beach."

"So actually, we're all pretty busy," I said.

"Yeah," Kareem said with a shrug. "Too bad."

There's a Methodist church camp in the mountains that I sort of wanted to go to. Canoeing and mountain-bike riding. Big hikes to waterfalls. Zip line. Mom hadn't signed me up yet. I didn't know if we could afford it, so I didn't push the idea. Fact was, I was happy to stay close by and do a little lake fishing and see Mignon at the swimming pool and hang out with her. There were all kinds of day hikes she and I could do together nearby. She knows a lot about birds and could teach me about that. But maybe she was going to some kind of camp, too. Parents love to send their kids to camp for a few weeks so they can relax.

"If Mignon will cut you loose, maybe we could go to the movies next weekend," Micky suggested.

"Yeah, let's do that." Kareem was in.

"Okay," I said. I knew I should see my friends more often, but I didn't for one reason or another. It was getting harder and harder to get together.

■

These days were all about the Time Box. (Notice I put it in capital letters.) I wanted to get it done.

Mignon asked if I was going to put in anything about movies or TV. That would be hard, because I'm not too into TV. I'll watch "The Simpsons" sometimes or some crazy stunt show, or sit down with Dad and watch some sports. But that's about it. (I do roam around on You Tube but that's hard to include.) We have three TV sets: a small one in the kitchen, a big one in the family room, and another medium one in Mom and Dad's bedroom. We considered the little kitchen TV Mom's. She watches Oprah and stuff like that on the tiny screen. Ella basically controls the big TV in the afternoon. She's limited in how much time she can watch and what she can watch. Anyway, she likes her regular kids shows, where the girls scream and the boys get punked. She watches something called "Memphis Police Women," when she can find it. But what she really likes are shows about animals. Orangutangs, porcupines, meerkats. It doesn't matter. She and Jake will sit on the couch together and watch. It keeps both of them quiet and out of mischief, which is a good thing. But there wasn't anything from TV that I wanted to put in my Box.

As for movies, well, I see a lot of them, but usually they're just an excuse to get out of the house and go to the mall. So I don't remember much of what I've seen. The one movie I want to put in the box is "Up." I really liked it, and I found the DVD in the bargain box of a video store that was going out of business. So that goes in. I liked "Guardians of the Galaxy" but I think that future people might just think it's silly.

Video games are a different story. I play games a lot, but I'm not putting any of them in the Time Box. They're still in action. I took the covers off a couple of the game boxes and tossed them in. I think anyone who finds them will figure out what they're about and how the games worked.

The next thing to include had to do with food. I'm sure whoever digs up the Time Box will be interested in what I liked to eat. The first thing I put in was Mom's recipe and I marked the envelope "Mom's Great Lasagna." Then I got a few menus. On the one from Andy's Pizza, I highlighted and circled my favorite pizza: "The Vesuvius." On the menu from Shanghai Garden, I circled Kung Pao Chicken and "Special Spring Rolls a la Danny". And last but not least, on the menu from The Barbecue Shack I just wrote "I like everything." That covered food. Too bad I couldn't include actual food, so that people could taste it thousands of years from now, but the recipe will help. They can try to make that lasagna themselves. Good luck to them.

▪

The box was filling up pretty good. Mignon came over. Her soccer season was over, too. They had reached the quarter finals but lost in a shootout, when Brenda Banks missed her shot. Mignon had a bruise on her leg where she'd been kicked. "Those girls were pretty rough," she said with a smile.

"I hope you kicked her back."

"Would I do that?" And I knew she had. She was eyeing the Box.

"Can I look?"

"Sure."

She pulled the box towards her and smiled when she saw the menus. "I love Shanghai's egg rolls and the orange chicken," she said. She picked up an object. "What's this?"

"It's a Tar Heel bottle opener. You open a bottle with it and it plays the Tar Heel fight song."

She picked up the baseball that the team had signed and given me after the big win over Concord. She tossed it to me.

"You should keep this."

Then she picked up my old Carolina t-shirt. It was blue with white letters: "If God isn't a Tar Heel, why is the sky Carolina blue?"

"You wore this all last summer," she said.

"Yeah."

"Sure you want to give it up?"

"I've almost outgrown it."

She put it back. There were a couple of interesting shells from the beach. When she pulled out an old tooth-brush, I said, "They need to know about our hygiene."

"Where's your story?" she asked.

"The one I did for English?"

"Yeah."

"I didn't put that in," I said.

She made a face. "You have to. That's important. Is it on your computer?"

"Yep."

"Well, print it now. And put it on a CD, too."

"I don't know."

"It's you—the real you—more than what you eat or listen to."

I did as I was told. I printed a copy and put that into an envelope, which she marked with a ballpoint, "Tommy's Story." She wrote the same thing with a Sharpie on the CD, and I put them both in the Time Box.

"You really think I need both?"

"If they don't have the right operating system, they might not be able to read it right away."

"Okay."

Suddenly Mignon looked nervous. She shook her head, as if something were rattling inside. "Hey. I'm sorry," she said. "I shouldn't tell you what to put in there."

"I don't mind, really."

"I promised myself that I wouldn't intrude."

"Well, there's a way you can help me."

"How?"

"I need to take your picture. I took photos of Kareem and Micky already."

"You want to take it now?"

"Tomorrow at the park. Our regular meeting place."

Again, like many times before, Mignon started to say something and then didn't.

"Going home," she said finally.

"I'll walk you."

"No. You stay here and work on your project. I'll be fine."

"The first part's almost over."

"See ya."

I heard her say goodbye to Mom. The door shut and she was gone. Digging through some old stuff, I found the rubber SpongeBob model that my grandparents had sent me from Florida a few years ago. I dumped it in the box. That should freak people out pretty good. I just hope whoever finds it doesn't think I was worshipping this strange yellow figure, but I guess that could happen.

I was feeling pretty good about my Time Box but I did put the baseball back on my bookshelf.

▪

I met Mignon in the park on Saturday morning to take her picture. She was wearing shorts and a funky tie-dyed t-shirt. Her green Keds covered up her painted toe nails. I posed her by the picnic table where we usually meet. Then I had her stand under one of the dogwoods, so that the blossoms seemed to grow around her head.

"Let me see," she asked.

I showed her the five pictures I'd taken and she shrugged.

"Maybe I should have worn something nicer."

"No, you look fine. You look like yourself."

"If you say so."

"How about I take a video of you?" I suggested.

"Doing what?"

"I don't know—maybe running. You look good running."

"Naw. That's weird."

"What's weird about it?"

"I don't know. It makes me feel uncomfortable."

I wanted to see if I could catch on a video how graceful she looked.

"All right, forget it."

She stared at me for a long moment. Mr. Parker was walking Mitzi on the sidewalk by the park. He was staring at me, too.

"What do you want me to do?" Mignon asked all of a sudden.

"Just go over by the creek. I'll say 'go' and you run up to the basketball court."

Four guys I didn't know were playing two on two at the court. It was an intense but friendly game. Mignon walked to the creek and turned back to me. I got the video ready. "Go!" I shouted.

Mignon fell into an easy jog along the creek bank, past a jungle gym, past a holly bush, and then she really started running, kicking up pine straw. So graceful. Beautiful. I was having a hard time following her on the phone. And she didn't stop at the court. She kept running. The basketball guys stopped playing and watched her.

"Go, girl!" one of them yelled.

Mignon ran past Mitzi, who started barking and lunging, wanting to chase her. Mr. Parker looked irritated. She ran past the Millikens' house on the corner and then disappeared. I turned off the video and sat down. Maybe she was embarrassed or something. Who knows? Micky says girls can suddenly do all kinds of weird things. Maybe she just ran home. Maybe she had to pee. I played back the video. Her long legs were stretching out and her hair was flying. When she started going faster the picture started bouncing and the focus was going in and out. It was kind of interesting.

"Yo, stretch it out!" one of the ball players shouted.

I looked up and saw Mignon heading straight towards me at full speed. I reached out and stopped her before she fell into the picnic table.

"Whoa! Thanks!" she said, trying to catch her breath. Her eyes were red. She rubbed her fists against them.

"Where'd you go?"

"Just around the block up there. Once I started running, I liked the feeling so I just kept going. I don't know why, but I just needed to keep going." She looked at me and shrugged. "Maybe I'll do track next year. Did I say that before?"

I nodded. "Mr. Dotson—they say he's a good track coach."

"Yeah. How's the video?" she asked.

"Good. Have a look."

She sat on the bench and I played it for her. At first, I couldn't tell whether she liked it or not. "You can hear the sound, too. That's great," she said.

Yes, you could hear her running and later hear the basketball bouncing and then the guy calling to her. "Very artistic, Tommy," she said.

"Thank you."

She was breathing normal again. Now she was studying me. "Your turn now."

"For what?" I asked.

"To make a video of you just telling about yourself."
Now it was my turn to be uncomfortable. "I'll take the
phone and you just start talking."

"I don't know what to say."

"Just imagine somebody has dug up the box and
figured out how to play a DVD or a CD. You have to
explain why you made the box and who you are."

"I don't know."

"C'mon. I ran. You just stand still and talk."

Even though the idea made sense, it felt weird. I
handed her the phone.

"Stand by the bush that you pushed me into. The
light's good there."

"I didn't push you," I said. "I tackled you."

She studied the controls on the phone for a moment.

"You know how to work it?" I asked.

She gave me a funny look. "Duh. It's just like my
phone. Get ready."

"I'm getting my thoughts collected." I wanted more
time, but she made a funny signal with her left hand for
me to start talking. I started but stopped after "hello"
when my voice broke. We both laughed and then I tried
again.

"Hello. My name is Tommy Johnson. I'm twelve years
old. I'll be thirteen in a couple of months: July twenty-sec-
ond, two thousand thirteen. If you're looking at this,
you've discovered my Time Box." I was really nervous
about what I should say. I sighed and fidgeted.

"Anyway, the reason I made this box was to let you
know that I was here in America, on the planet Earth, at

this time and that I was happy here. I wanted someone in the future—either a human like me or an alien from some other galaxy—to know what it was like to be me in this time and in this place. I wanted you to know some of the things that I like and how nice life was, or is—not just for me but for other people, too.

You know, in the United States, we're free to try to be whatever we want to be. Of course, I haven't started that yet but I hope to do something good that helps people. I'm only in the seventh grade. So even if I never become something great, Tommy Johnson is a real person, an ordinary person, with a good family and good friends. I can't think of any place I'd rather be right now than here. I hope you enjoy the music and the books and the other stuff I've put in the box. And please try to make the lasagna. I think you'll love it. Thanks for your attention. Bye."

Mignon stopped recording and I let out a big sigh.

"That was great," she said.

"I got so nervous."

"I couldn't tell. Much." Her red eyes were gone.

Suddenly I felt tired. It was as if somebody put big weights on my head and shoulders.

"Let's go to my house," she said. "Mom will make us a couple of smoothies and we can play some Mario."

I couldn't turn down that invitation. The smoothies would be great and Mario's fun. And Pierre was at the dog groomer.

■

Excuse me, but I'm going to meander again. I have to say I love my phone. I guess everybody does. Think about it. I can keep contact with my friends anywhere as long as I or someone pays the bill. I can take photos and make videos with it. (Like I did.) I can store and play music and games. I can watch TV shows and movies. I can research stuff about anything and get info from anywhere. When I have a credit card some day, I can buy things with it. It even can keep me from getting lost. It's amazing that somebody invented it and it keeps getting better. It's probably the best invention that I've ever known. Better than the airplane or the car or air-conditioning.

▪

That night I watched my video. I sure looked jittery. My eyes moved all around. Sometimes I'd be looking at the trees or the ground. Sometimes I'd look right at Mignon, and then look to the side. Of course, you never think you look like you do.

"I look so dorkie," I said to Mignon during our pre-sleep FaceTime.

"No, you don't." Her face filled the screen. "You're not going to dump it, are you?"

I'd been considering trashing it. My silence was her answer.

"You want me to say it. Is that what you want? You were cute. And I liked what you said. I'm being totally honest. You have to put in in the box."

"I thought you didn't want to—what was your word?—*intrude*."

"I don't, but when you're being crazy...."

"I'm beginning to think this whole thing is crazy." I paused and I could see her stressing and getting angry. "Well, I already put it in the Box. It's almost full."

She finally smiled. "Good night, Tommy."

"Good night, Mignon."

I rolled back on my bed. Was there anything I still needed to put in the Time Box? And how was I going to make the real Box?

CHAPTER FIFTEEN

FTER CHURCH AND after I cut the grass at home, I walked up to Dr. Bugg's house. He was working on something in his garage. I could hear the saw buzzing. He knew a lot about building stuff. He could help. But standing at the end of his driveway, I got a little nervous and decided not to interrupt him. As I turned to go home, he saw me.

"Thomas, what are you up to?"

"Nothing much. How about you, Dr. Bugg?" I walked up to the garage.

"I'm starting on a whirligig. I'm gonna do a little wood one first and then do a bigger one in metal. All about bugs, moving around. I could use a young guy's imagination to help me think it out."

"I don't know if I could help you."

I'd seen a couple of whirligigs. They were on a hill overlooking the walking trail that surrounded the art museum. I think they both were made of metal, but I wasn't sure. When the wind blew, they moved all kinds of ways.

"Well, I'd appreciate your opinion once it starts taking shape," he said.

"Sure." I had a short opening. "How about making one in plastic?"

Dr. Bugg stopped cold. He had what looked like a propeller in his hand. "Why do you say that?"

"One of my teachers said plastic lasts a long time. Since your whirligig might be outdoors in the wind and rain that might be good."

"See. You've already come in handy with a new idea," he said.

"Is it hard to work with plastic?" I asked.

"It depends." He gave me a quick look. "Are you planning something?"

"Yes, sir. There's something I wanted to build, but I don't know if I can. A kind of a box." I tried to show the size with my hands.

"Is it an aquarium or something like that?" Dr. Bugg asked.

There are moments when your brain stops and a door opens that wasn't there before. You can walk right through that door. "You guessed it. An aquarium. I love fish," I lied.

"Well, that will be a little harder than building a box, because it's got to hold water and weight. Water weighs a lot. So how you put it together is real important."

"But could I do it?"

"I think so. With a little help. The adhesive has to be set up right. You'd use Plexiglas, I think. Acrylic would be good. Around a quarter-inch plexi. Maybe less."

Dr. Bugg was thinking out loud. "How big do you want it?" he continued.

I hadn't measured exactly, but it had to be the size of the cardboard one. "I'm thinking it should be about this long." I held out my hands.

"About a foot?"

"If that's a foot, then let's say ten inches high and wide." I remembered there were a couple of tens on the side of the box.

"That's a reasonable size. You're going to have to get the plexi cut to your dimensions and then glue them together."

He went to his work bench and drew out a picture of the aquarium box.

"That's exactly what I had in mind," I said, studying his drawing.

"So you just go to a plastic company, have them cut this, and they'll sell you the proper adhesive. You just tell them what you're going to do with it. The water element and all. Probably got to clamp it down."

This was sounding harder and harder. "Great," I said. "Can I have the drawing?"

Dr. Bugg nodded and I took it. "And I'm sure your Dad can help you on this?" he asked.

"Well, I'd kinda like to keep him in the dark; plus he's working on his car."

"Is it a gift for him?" Dr. Bugg asked, with a wink.

"I'm hoping."

That door was now wide open and the sun seemed to

be shining through.

"Well, when it comes to putting it together, I'll be glad to help."

"I'd be glad to cut your grass in return," I said.

"That's a good trade."

"Thanks for the advice and the drawing."

"You're totally welcome."

I turned for home. My cheeks were burning. I'd lied in several big ways. Would I get in trouble? Would Dr. Bugg come looking for the aquarium one day?

■

In my room that night, I studied the drawing. I needed four sheets that were twelve inches by ten inches. That's the top and bottom and then two sides. And two more that were ten by ten. The ends of the box. How much would they cost? I had money I'd saved from my allowance and selling old video games. Would that be enough? Where would I buy the stuff? It's not like they sell it at Home Depot or Lowe's.

"I've got some money I can loan you," Mignon said. "I've got close to 30. I did one babysitting job next door and they gave me twenty dollars. It was just for the dog—not a real baby."

"I hope I don't need it, but thanks for offering."

"Your project is now making ME tense," she said.

"You're tense? I'm in a knot. I just lied to my nice neighbor."

"It wasn't a mean lie."

"I'm not sure I can build it even if I can get the stuff.

It's harder than I thought. Maybe the whole thing is just stupid." I paused, waiting for her to say something.

"You can't give up now," she said, looking straight in my face.

"I don't want to, but...."

"Maybe you could make it out of something else."

"Whatever I make it out of, it's going to take a lot of work and money."

"Just sleep on it," she suggested.

"Yeah. Maybe something will come to me in a dream."

She smiled. "Stop it. You look so depressed."

"I am depressed. Mainly about lying."

"See you tomorrow." Her voice was soft and sleepy.

"Good night."

I turned off the phone and just laid there on my bed. I had to get this all straightened quick or else I wouldn't be able to study for the end-of-term tests. I wouldn't be worth anything.

▪

The next day at school I walked around in a fog, barely paying attention to anything around me. Mignon had a student council meeting and I walked home with Kareem.

"I'm getting weirded out, man," Kareem said.

"Over what?"

"Pressure. It's crazy. This basketball thing is getting outta hand."

"How so?" I asked.

He shook his head.

"My mom. She's all over me. And Uncle Taylor and my

cousin, Double G. I'm in the seventh grade and they're all over me."

"About school?"

"Yeah, but really about basketball. They're the ones who got me in these camps. I'm glad to go, but it's getting big. And Double G comes over on weekends and works on me at the Y or the park. He played some junior-college ball. He says he wants to toughen me up. Crap."

"You'll get to see some players in Chapel Hill. Tyler. Lawson. The pros. Barnes."

"That's the good part. Being in that gym. Love Ty. He's my man."

When we reached the park, Kareem went straight to the basketball court and shot a few layups. I made a shot or two, and then it was obvious that the shooting calmed him down, so I just fed him while he took jumps shots. Most of them snapped the net perfectly. Swish. Swish.

"I love basketball. Really. I'm good at it and I can get better, but I can feel people looking at me now, and that's how they see me. The future big basketball star. Even my family. I guess that won't change."

"Should it?"

"I'm still a kid. But Double G told me last week, they start recruiting you in eighth grade if you're any count. So next year college coaches might start showing up at the gym."

"Some people would think that's cool," I said. "Me included."

"Sure. But I don't see you and Micky enough as it is. I don't see Latitia as much as I'd like. My Uncle Taylor said,

'That girl can ruin your life, boy. You gotta be smart.' What the hell does that mean? I'd just like to spend some time laying around and being a kid. I start feeling that I'm working for them: my mom, Uncle Taylor, Double G. I know they think they're helping me, but I play basketball because it's fun. Straight up fun. When I'm playing, I used to not think about any troubles, but now, other things come in my head. What happens if I get injured or something? What happens then?"

"Me and Micky will come see you in the hospital. Bring you some Double Mints."

He stood at the foul line, the basketball tucked under his arm, and laughed. "Yeah, I can see that."

"Everybody stresses about something," I said, thinking about the Time Box.

▪

It took a couple of days for me to work up the nerve to do what was necessary. Dr. Bugg was finishing up his first whirligig. "Hey, Thomas. How's your project going?"

"That's what I want to talk to you about."

He could see how nervous and serious I was. He stopped and put his hands on his hips. "What is it?" he asked.

I hesitated, then let it out.

"I lied to you."

"You did?"

"Yes, sir, and I'm sorry. I apologize. I'm not trying to build any aquarium. That's a lie." My knees were weak.

He studied me. "Are you trying to build anything?"

"Yes, sir."

"What is it?" he asked. He had a very serious look.

"It's hard to describe." This wasn't going to be fun.

"Come in and sit down."

I went inside the garage shop and he pushed out a little stool for me to sit on. He sat on an old wooden chair that he might have made himself. "I appreciate your coming and apologizing. It happens some times that you get caught up in something. Everybody does."

"Yes, sir."

"So, what's the story?"

"You're gonna think I'm crazy, but I want to build a time capsule thing. Really a Time Box."

"A Time Box." He stared at me for a long time. "Something you're gonna put away or bury?"

"Yes, sir. That's the idea."

Was he smiling?

"What you gonna put in it?" Another big question.

"Just dumb stuff. My stuff from right now." I suddenly felt stupid and crazy at the same time, but I thought that I might as well put it all out there. "I want to bury something that somebody might dig up a long time from now and know I was here, and how it was."

"How what was?" he asked.

"Life. My life at twelve. That's it." I wanted to bolt and run down the street and hope Dr. Bugg wouldn't say anything to anybody. He rocked back in his chair for a moment. "I think that's a hell of a good idea," he said.

Suddenly it seemed sunny again. "You do?"

"I do. I get it. A Time Box. And I'd be glad to help you.

After the other day, I thought, how is that boy going to build an aquarium by himself? The process will be tough and cost money. Even a small aquarium that you buy in the pet store could cost a hundred dollars or more."

"Wow."

"I'll help you, but you'll have to work with me on it. And I'm taking you up on the grass cutting and you'll have to pay for the materials. But I'll get them for you. Is it a deal?" He stuck out his huge, rough hand.

"Yes, sir," I said and shook his hand as strong as I could. "Thank you."

It's hard to explain how I felt, trotting back home that day. There are times when you think some older person or your parents are going to smack your ideas down or make fun of you, but then they don't. They understand you in a way that you thought they couldn't. That's a big thing to understand. I couldn't wait to tell Mignon what happened.

■

The first thing I did for my deal with Dr. Bugg was cut his grass. He gave me a tip of five dollars for sweeping up, and with the thirty-seven I already had, I was able to cover all the materials plus the glue—adhesive, he called it. Thank God I didn't have to borrow from Ella. She would have charged me interest and then blabbed the whole thing to Mom and Dad.

After the grass cutting I went into the garage and saw the Plexiglas on his work table. There were six pieces a little under a quarter of an inch thick. The base. Two long side pieces. Two short side pieces. The top.

"Here's your receipt and some change," Dr. Bugg said.

I put the money and the paper in my back pocket.

"Ready to go to work?" he asked.

"Yes, sir."

Dr. Bugg had me sand a portion of the base where the sides would be attached. That's where I started. He then had me softly sand two side pieces where they would connect. In the meantime he was pouring a clear concoction into a little plastic bottle. This was the adhesive stuff. Then he put a needle in the bottle so that it looked like one of those hypodermics they give you shots with at the doctor's office.

"Okay, Thomas, you've got to hold that piece. Right there."

I took a big breath and held the plastic. He squeezed the adhesive where the side pieces met the base. I held tight. While we were waiting for this first part to set up, Dr. Bugg started to ask questions.

"How'd did you get this idea?"

"Well, my friend Mignon put it in my mind, and then it just seemed like I had to do it."

"Have you picked the things you're putting in it?"

"Yes, sir. It's just stuff that tells people what I like to do or what I think about."

"You know where you might put it or bury it?"

"Don't know yet. I have to figure out a place that's safe."

Dr. Bugg rubbed his knee as if it was sore. "You want people in the future to know about you, is that right?"

"Yes, sir. See, I was thinking if I got sick or had an accident and died, nobody would ever know I was here and they wouldn't know what I liked or what life was like for me. Tommy Johnson would be like one of your bugs. Here today; gone tomorrow."

Dr. Bugg took a deep breath. "I remember when you came by in the fall you were, well, stressed out about the big universe."

"Still am. The universe makes you feel smaller than small. You want at least to leave something behind besides your bones. I mean, a few people become famous and people remember them for a while, but in a thousand years they won't even know what the famous people were like. What they thought about or felt—nothing personal at all."

Dr. Bugg nodded four or five times, like thoughts were rattling in his head. "You're doing a lot of deep thinking."

"I don't mean to."

He checked the plexi. The adhesive seemed to have set okay. "We'll let this sit tonight. I'll clamp it and then we'll start again tomorrow with the other sides. The longer it cures, the better."

"See you then. By the way, how's the whirligig?"

"Look over by that magnolia."

The whirligig was set on a post. It seemed to be made up of a bunch of bugs that were swirling around as the propeller turned in the breeze. A lady bug and a beetle danced with a moth.

"Looks great!" I shouted and headed home.

▪

Mignon and I had lunch outside, sitting under the crepe myrtle tree that was promising to bloom soon.

"So how is it?" she asked.

"It's going good. Maybe in two days we'll be done."

"You're kidding?"

"No. Dr. Bugg, he understands the idea and he can build anything."

"So when can you put the stuff in?"

"Like I said. A couple of days."

She took a small bite of her taco.

"After I fill it up, then I just put the top on and that's it."

"I can't believe it's really happening." She was excited.

"Me, neither."

"Does anybody know besides you and me and Dr. Bugg?"

"Nope."

Mignon rocked back, shaking her head.

"Are you gonna finish that taco?" I asked her.

"No. I can't eat."

I grabbed the taco and gobbled it down. Jeannie sauntered over. "Hello, love birds," she said.

My cue to leave.

"I'll text you later," I said.

"Nice seeing you, too, Tommy," Jeannie said.

My mind was spinning. I couldn't wait to get back to the garage with Dr. Bugg. What made it nicer was that Mignon was as excited as I was.

■

At dinner that night, Dad's curiosity slipped out. "You're getting pretty tight with Dr. Bugg," he said.

"Yes, sir."

"He teaching you about insects and such?"

"He's teaching me about building stuff. It's fun. He's making whirligigs. I'm just helping out."

"That's interesting. He gave us that birdhouse on the patio last Christmas."

"I know. He does talk a little bit about bugs. If we see one crawling on the floor, he knows all about it. Knows its name in Latin. All that stuff. Knows what it eats and how it fits into nature."

"Well, I'm sure he likes your company. You know his wife is very ill," Mom added, dishing out some more mashed potatoes.

"I haven't seen her," I said.

"She doesn't get out much. In the morning, he sometimes walks her out to the sidewalk and back a couple of times. Or he sits her in the backyard if it's sunny. They say she's losing her memory. Ella, please stop playing with your food."

Ella had made a kind of animal sculpture from the mashed potatoes. It looked like a hippo. "I really don't like mashed potatoes," she said.

"You finish your food, Ella," Dad said in his most serious voice.

Ella dipped her fork in the mound and took a taste and scrunched her face up.

"I would think it'd be terrible to lose your memory," I

said. I really meant that. "Who are you if you don't even know your name or the names of your parents and the town you live in? Or if you don't remember the things you learned in school or the feelings you have for your friends?"

"Some memories people want to forget," Dad said.

"Seems like you can't pick and choose what you remember or forget when you have that illness," Mom said with a sigh. "Things just get erased."

Upstairs, I looked back through the old cardboard box and the things that I'd stuffed in it lately: The church program from Uncle Aaron's funeral. A photo I'd printed off the Internet of the Crab Nebula, where stars were being born. Photos of Jake and Ella; Mom and Dad; Kareem and Micky; our house. I'd printed the pictures of Mignon (she looked goofy in a couple and really pretty in the others) and put them on top of everything. I don't know how long the prints will last, but all the pictures were on a DVD, too.

I labelled most everything with a black Sharpie. This was it. This was my Time Box.

▪

The next day we finished the final sides of the box. After waiting another day for the box to cure (Dr. Bugg's word), I went over to his house after school. There it was on his work table. The Time Box.

"I'm sure you can finish it up, Thomas," Dr. Bugg said. "You know how to do it. Just don't be impatient. The adhesive sets up real fast, but the longer it sits, the better the weld. When you get that top on good, you'll be able to stand on it. For sure. That's how strong it is."

I picked up the box. It wasn't light. Dr. Bugg had put the two cans of the adhesive inside along with the needled bottle he called the "syringe."

"Thank you, sir, for everything. It means a lot to me."

"You're welcome."

"And I hope Mrs. Bugg gets better. Mom said she's been sick for a while."

He just nodded like he was deep-thinking. I could feel his eyes on me as I walked down the driveway with the box.

"Tommy, keep me up to date," he called. "Tell me if it works out."

"Sure will," I promised. That was the first time he'd ever called me Tommy.

CHAPTER SIXTEEN

WHEN I GOT home I knew that Ella would either be watching TV for her 30-minute school-night permit or working her DS. Either way, she'd be in a fog. Mom would be making dinner. I yelled, "I'm home!" as I banged through the door and speed-jumped up the stairs to my room.

"Everything okay?" Mom called up.

"Yep." Then I came out of my room to ask her a question. "Hey, Mom, can Mignon come over for dinner tonight?"

A long pause. Maybe she was checking whether we had enough food.

"Sure. Dad's going to a men's meeting at the church tonight and he'll have dinner there."

"How long before we eat?" I asked.

"Twenty or thirty minutes."

I texted Mignon. "Come to dinner? 20 minutes. The box is here."

She answered. "OMG. Yes."

Dinner went quick. Mom had made her lemon chicken and that's always tasty. Mignon seemed to like it. Even Ella ate everything on her plate. Mom and Mignon did most of the talking at the dinner table, as usual. Mom wanted to know about school and did Mignon have plans for college. (She did.) Mignon thought she might like to keep working on her art and they talked about that for a while. Jake sat right next to Ella, hoping that she'd either hand him something she didn't want to eat or drop something accidentally. I didn't want to seem too eager to finish up, but I was jittery.

"Do you need to go to the bathroom or something, son?" Mom asked.

In self-defense, I answered, "Yes, ma'am. Excuse me."

I went to the bathroom and stood there, looking in the mirror. Of course, if you go into a bathroom, eventually you'll have to pee even if you didn't need to before. When I came back to the dining room, Ella and Mignon were helping Mom clear the table.

"Mignon said she needs some help with her science work.," Mom said.

"Yes, she sure does. Let's get started."

We rushed upstairs.

"I knew you wanted to get up here, so I had to say something," she whispered.

"Good thinking."

We closed the door and I showed her the box. She touched it and then lifted it a few inches off the floor. "Wow! That looks great."

"What I want to do now is load everything in it and

close it up. You'll have to help me with the top."

"Okay. You just have to tell me what to do."

I had brought up some old newspaper and spread it on the floor, in case something spilled. I put the box in the middle of the newspaper. "I don't have to mix anything," I told her. "It's just in this can." I poured some of the adhesive stuff into the little plastic bottle and then attached the needle top.

"The stuff looks like water," Mignon said.

"Yeah."

"What do I need to do?" she asked.

"First, I put the glue on the ends. Then you're gonna set the top down so it matches up and you keep it from moving. Then I squirt more adhesive on the edge. It seals up real quick."

"That's it?"

I nodded. "But let's put the stuff in it first," I said.

Mignon picked up the pictures of herself on the top of the pile and gave me a look.

"You want to put all of them in there? This one's real dorkie." She held up a picture where she was acting shy.

"No, I like it and it's my Time Box."

Putting things in the new box seemed like a ritual that you might see in a church where they have big rituals. Should I say Catholics? I would take things out and hand them to Mignon, who carefully placed them in the Time Box. She was really focused.

"Keep this up and you can get a job at the Teeter bagging groceries," I said.

"You want to do this right, don't you?" she asked.

"That was a compliment. Relax."

Soon everything was in the box, or so I thought.

"Before you close it up, I have something," Mignon said.

She grabbed the soft bag that she'd brought with her, reached inside, and pulled out a drawing pad. She opened it and held it up for me to see. It was a picture, drawn in pencil, of me sitting on the picnic table down at the park. Above me, in the sky, she had drawn stars and planets and meteors streaking past night clouds. It was a great picture, and at the bottom she had signed, "Love Mignon 2013."

"I'd like to put that in there, unless you don't like it," she said.

"No, it's great. I like it a lot. But do you really want to put it in the box? Nobody will see it for maybe hundreds or thousands of years."

"Exactly. You have photos of me in there. Maybe they'd like to see what I do, or what I did."

She had a point. "Okay. It's really great, Mignon. Thanks."

How had she drawn that from her memory—my crazy hair, the one broken leg of the bench? I sat back on the bed as she placed the drawing in the box. She looked up now, waiting for the next move.

"Okay, let's do it," I said.

"Okay."

"You just fit it on the top exactly like I told you and I'll do the rest. Any questions?"

No questions. And I was sure that she knew what she

needed to do. I aimed the needle. Not too much and not too little, like Dr. Bugg said. Mignon moved seriously. She stood over the box so she had a good view of the angles. Slowly and steadily, she lowered the top on to the box. The adhesive stuff leaked into the seam. One small adjustment of the edges. A perfect fit. We both exhaled and then the door busted open and Ella was standing there with her DS in her hand.

"What are you guys doing? Tommy, what's that in your hand?"

We froze. I was holding the syringe.

"Nothing."

"Are you guys doing drugs? That thing looks like what people on TV use to put drugs in their arms."

"It's not drugs. It's glue."

"Glue? What are you doing with it?" she asked suspiciously.

"School project," I told her.

"I thought gluing stuff would be over by seventh grade."

"No way," I said.

"Ella, they even glue in eighth grade," Mignon added.

"Dang! That's depressing. Bye."

She exited. I got up and closed the door. Mignon laughed. "Maybe you could play some music or something."

"Like the Lumineers?" I asked.

"Yeah, okay."

I put the volume on my phone at the highest level. Mignon gave me a wink.

"I belong with you, you belong with me, you're my sweet heart." Wish that were true.

I don't think I could live very long without music. If I was lost in the forest I'd sing a made-up song or beat on a tree trunk like a drum. Maybe Otzi liked to sing up in the mountains. Maybe he could yodel. When I was running cross-country I'd hum a song. It kept me going. No wonder armies had marching bands.

Mignon still had her hands pressing down on the top of the box.

"Want to take a break?" I asked.

She shrugged. It had been a few minutes. "Don't I need to press it down?"

"No, it's set already. We just need to let it sit for a while."

Mignon picked up my iPhone and started rolling through my music, looking for something to play. "Don't feel like Fun or the Granules," she said. "I'll go back up. Who are the Dips?"

"They're from here. Over in Durham. I only have two of their songs. "Grits and Gravy" is good. Then there's their love song, 'Salmonella.'"

She laughed. "How about some Beatles?" she asked.

"Okay."

Mignon chose "All You Need is Love."

"I think it's ...appropriate," she said.

And it was. The Beatles session went on for another two songs and then I studied the box and seams.

"Is it done, really?" Mignon asked.

"I think so."

"That's it? It's sealed up?"

"Yeah."

"I can't believe it," she said in a whisper.

We were both just staring at each other and then at the box when I heard Dad's truck pull into the drive.

"I should go now," she said.

"But first...."

"What?" she asked.

I took Mignon's hand and led her to the box. "Let's see how heavy it is," I said. I lifted it up. It wasn't real heavy, but if you had to carry it a long way, it could get tough. I handed it to Mignon.

"It's not so heavy," she said. She carefully set the box back on the floor.

"Stand up on it," I told her.

"Are you crazy?" she asked.

"Dr. Bugg said you could do it."

She hesitated, then carefully put one foot up. Pressing my shoulder, she lifted the other foot until she was standing on the box.

"Hold it." I took a quick photo of her standing nervously on top of the Time Box. The flash made her blink.

"Can I get off now?"

I nodded and she jumped down.

"Now what?" she asked.

"Got to figure where it gets buried."

"How about your backyard?"

I shook my head. "Naw. It needs to be somewhere that people or aliens will likely dig it up. Somewhere important, kind of."

"Well, I got to go." She headed for the door.

"Thanks for helping. Nobody else could have done it."

"B.S.," she mouthed.

We walked downstairs. Dad was talking to Mom in the kitchen.

"Thanks for dinner, Mrs. Johnson," Mignon said.

"You're welcome, honey. Anytime."

Outside, the stars seemed lost in some clouds. The moon was just a dull glow behind the fog. Mignon had come over on her bike. She picked it up and I went over to her. I wanted to give her a hug like the ones Mom gives me. She was holding the bike when I put my arms around her.

"Thanks," I said again. "Thanks really."

"Thanks for including me," she said. There was her sad look again; then she jumped on her bike and started pedaling for home.

"See you tomorrow!" I shouted.

She waved and was gone.

▪

For the next couple of days, I thought about where to bury the Time Box.

I considered the Presbyterian Church near my house, but they had converted most of their land to a playground for kids. It was walled in. There wasn't space to dig that wouldn't be obvious.

Mignon suggested the school. There was a space by the gym between the gym wall and some evergreen trees that might work. But the more I thought about it, the more I realized that even if I got it in the ground, someone might notice new digging. The school had landscape people and they definitely would notice something new. Maybe they'd get curious and dig it up.

Meanwhile, everybody was beginning to make plans for summer. Jacob was going to a Jewish camp in Pennsylvania. David was doing a Boy Scout camp. Micky was still planning.

"Now Dad wants me to go to golf camp for a week. I hate golf. It's a stupid sport, but since Tiger Woods is half Thai or something, Dad thinks Asians have a gift for golf. I say, if you're going to play a sport, play one that attracts girls. Golf doesn't attract girls. What's up for you?"

"I don't know what I'm going to do. Dad wants me to work on my baseball and help him with the car. Mom wants me to work on my math." I was stalling.

"You know, you could come to the beach when we rent the house. The place has about eight bedrooms. Duncan is bringing his girlfriend and you could bring Mignon. We have rafts and surfboards. Fishing poles."

"You think that could work out?" I asked.

"Sure. It would be great."

The bell rang for class. Mignon came by as we went down the hall. She wanted to talk.

"I keep thinking. You know, it has to be a place where people, the archae—" She was searching for the word.

"Archaeologists."

"Right. Where the archaeologists like to dig. In Rome, there's the Forum. Don't give me that smirk. I looked it up in the library. Or in Athens, they found the center of town, where people congregated. The Agora, it's called. Lots of old buildings and streets. Actually, I think it would be great to be an archaeologist and dig up ancient places. Think about it."

With that piece of advice, she was gone. She'd been doing some research. And all I could think of was being down at the beach with her, swimming and playing miniature golf. Just kidding about the miniature golf. Summer at the beach with Mignon would be great. Maybe Micky's folks would be okay with it. Maybe Mignon's Mom and Dad wouldn't say no if she had a friend going, like Jeannie or Brenda. At night the sky at the beach is so big. You can see so many stars and, if you're lucky, some falling ones to wish on. The truth was (and I've said it before) I'd be happy to be with Mignon anywhere. Even just hanging with her at the mall is good.

Boom. That's when the answer came to me, like a vision you read about in the Bible. Remember the burning bush?

"Tommy. Tommy!" Miss Tyler's loud voice woke me from my vision.

"Sorry," I said, sitting down at my desk. Mignon looked at me with a worried face. I mouthed, "I got it."

The mall. It was the mall. That's where people get together. That's where every kid I know hangs out. If the people of the future want to know how we lived, they'll have to dig up the malls. There are about five or six big malls around the city, and depending on what you want to do or where you live, you have to go to one or the other. One has bowling. One has a zip line. Three have movies. All have food courts.

And malls aren't just for kids. If you go to any big mall, just before the stores open, you'll see flocks of old people walking around. They walk from one end of the mall to the other, round and round. They all seem to wear good, new walking shoes and they don't walk slow. If you meander, you might get run over by an 80-year-old. They're getting their exercise in air-conditioned comfort. No rain or sleet or burning sun to worry about. And when they finish, they go to the food court and have breakfast. Cup of coffee, sausage biscuit—whatever. They sit around and chat. Maybe they hang around for a massage or a pedicure later.

The question was, where in any of these malls could you find a spot for the digging and burying?

▪

"At a mall? That's perfect," Mignon said, and then she had a second thought. "But which one, and where?"

"That's the big question."

We were sitting in our usual spot at the park. Mignon tossed me a Hershey's kiss. "Your brain needs some energy," she said.

I gobbled the chocolate. "The problem is, if we go to one of the big malls, someone would have to drive us, and I don't want to involve anyone else in my shenanigans."

"'Shenanigans'? Where'd you find that word?" she asked.

"I read it somewhere. It sounds like what it is. That

and 'concoction' are my two favorite new words of the year."

"So if you don't go to, say, Briercreek or Southpoint, then where?"

"I don't know. The other thing is, you got to find a place where you can dig an actual hole. It has to be pretty deep."

She shook her head. "Maybe the mall idea is too big a deal. Why don't you just bury it here in the park? We could dig for hours here and nobody would say anything."

That wasn't my first choice. The chances of the box being discovered here in the park wouldn't be good.

"I could bury it at my house, but chances are, my parents could get into it and Ella and Jake, too. That's not good, either."

"People are always digging at the cemetery," she suggested.

"It would be confusing if it was found there. Plus the big ones have all kinds of security."

"Not to mention the ghosts who don't want to be disturbed," she said, giving me a look.

I didn't know whether she was kidding or not.

"Well, I just have to think it through."

I was getting a little discouraged. After all this work, it was beginning to look like I might have to bury the Time Box somewhere out of the way, like the park. It would be easy to dig there, behind the old shelter where the soil was sandy.

Mignon gave me a shoulder punch. "How about Carleton or Greenhill?" she asked.

Those two places, Carleton Place and Greenhill Center, aren't exactly malls. They're called shopping centers and they're older and smaller. They're outdoors, with shops spread around, but they're also close to the neighborhood. We could walk there or ride our bikes. Neither place has a movie theater, but they do have restaurants and boutiques where girls like to shop. They have health-food stores and banks. One has a big grocery store. They both have drugstores. That kind of thing. They're good gathering places, with some green areas all around.

"One of those could work. Maybe," I said.

That night, Mignon and I talked about the end of school and the last tests we were studying for. We didn't mention the Time Box. The Time Box itself sat at the end of my bed, covered by my baseball jersey. Number fifty. I chose that number because it was Tyler Hansbrough's at UNC. He was a beast. He never gave up. Would I?

I had a hard time getting to sleep until Jake came up to my room. He stared at me for a minute, as if he knew I was thinking too hard. Finally, he decided I needed company, and he jumped in my bed and cuddled at my feet. Listening to his deep breaths relaxed me, and in a few minutes I was in dreamland.

▪

The next day, after my last test, I decided to go by Green-hill and Carleton after school. I went to Greenhill first, because it's furthest away. There was a long hill to bike up, and I thought, that would be hard if I was hauling the box. I didn't see much space for digging when I got there. It was mostly parking lot and its green area was next to the big road leading out of town. That road was never empty, so digging in the green area would not be possible. There was one little plot at the back entrance, but digging there might mean destroying an azalea or two.

I coasted back down the hill towards Carleton. My Mom shops there a lot, especially for groceries. It was getting late by the time I rode up. People were leaving work, so there was a lot of traffic. Carleton had the same problem as Greenhill—it's mostly parking lot. The more I thought about the box, the more I thought about how long it would take to dig a hole for it. At least an hour— maybe two. Maybe I could steal a backhoe or some other ridiculous equipment.

The whole project was getting too big and maybe impossible without involving other people. It was looking more like it would be the park or my backyard. Too bad. And then I saw some real digging.

Across the street from the grocery store, a new building was going up. I didn't remember what had been on this corner before, but whatever it was had been torn down and all the old materials hauled away. The new building looked almost finished. At least the outside walls were up. The lot was all red dirt with poles and markers in different places. There was a guy on a Bobcat doing something and another guy with a shovel, just digging. The lot was surrounded by a low fence. There was an orange plastic fence around some trees and bushes that

I guess they wanted to save. A "no trespassing" sign was nailed to a post.

I pedaled over to where the guy with the shovel was working. He seemed to be Latino. "Buenos dias," I said. I always knew that fifth-grade Spanish would come in handy one day.

"Dias," he said, crawling out of the hole he'd made. The hole looked about four feet deep.

"What's building here?" I hoped he spoke a little English.

He looked up.

"What's that building?" I asked again.

"It's gonna be bank."

"Oh, yeah. I was hoping it would be a Chick-fil-A."

He smiled and wiped his hands on his trousers. His boots were caked in red mud.

"What you digging for?"

"Looking for pipes."

"Find any?"

He shook his head. "Checking. I don't think the pipe is here. It's over there." He pointed to a spot about 20 feet away.

The guy on the Bobcat had shut it down and was leaving. He walked over to a group of workers by the building. They were laughing at something. The Latino man stretched his arms and took one more look down into the hole. That's when it started to drizzle a little. An old Ford double-cab pulled up and an amigo in the truck called to him. He looked up, nodded, and then dragged a piece of plywood over the hole to keep people from falling in. He must have thought I was crazy, because I kept watching him. He tossed the shovel on his shoulder and jumped in the truck, just as the drizzle got heavier.

In a few minutes everybody had left the lot. I was getting soaked as I rode home, but I didn't care. I was totally jacked up. This could be it, I thought. I pedaled like a demon. I had to tell Mignon. We probably just had this one night to do the deed or quit and bury the Time Box in the park.

CHAPTER SEVENTEEN

THERE COMES A time in any story when something out of the ordinary happens and changes the outcome. You know, like the prison guard falls asleep so the prisoners can escape or two people who don't know each other bump cars by accident, meet, and fall in love. You know what I mean. A piece of luck. This is what that hole was like. We could have never dug it out on our own, but now we had a chance to use it.

I FaceTimed Mignon. "I found a hole to put the box in at Carlton Place. But I have to use it tonight. If you can't go, it's okay. If you can, one a.m. in the park."

There was a long wait. "I don't know," she said.

"Don't worry about it."

"It's so sudden." She looked nervous.

"Yeah, it just happened. But we only have one night to get it done."

"Okay."

"Later."

"I'll try," she said, in a tone that said it wasn't likely to happen.

I went to the garage and found the old spade. I took some twine that Mom used for her plants and made a sling for it and then stowed it outside with my bike. The rain had finally stopped, and I went to bed like normal. But I didn't sleep a wink. Seven minutes before one, I got up and snuck down the stairs. Jake watched me from his dog bed but he didn't bark or anything. Holding the box under my arm with the spade hung over my back, I rode down to the park. It was real tricky to keep my balance. The street was empty and the park was dark, except for a street light on the corner that lit half the basketball court. At one o'clock there was no Mignon. I knew it would be tough carrying the box and pedaling by myself. Just getting to the park had been hard. I might have to stop once or twice on the way, but I didn't have any other choice. I pushed off. As I started on my mission, Mignon came running down the street.

"I couldn't get my bike out of the garage," she whispered.

"That's okay."

"If my folks find out I'm gone, they'll freak. They'll have alerts on TV."

"You don't have to go," I said. "I don't want you to get in trouble."

"I left a note on my bed."

"Saying what?"

"That I wasn't kidnapped or running away. I'd be back soon."

"You think that would stop them from freaking?"

"Nope," she said, laughing.

"Like I said, you can go home."

"You think we can really do this?" she asked. She was catching her breath; waiting for me to answer.

"Yeah, I'm pretty sure. But we need to get started. I don't want to get caught, either."

"So what should I do?"

"You ride on the handlebars and hold the box. That's how we have to do it."

"Okay."

Mignon didn't hesitate. I handed her the Time Box and off we went. It wasn't going to be easy for her to keep her balance on the bars and hold that box. She could lean her head back against my chest, and that would help. It was a tough pedal for the first couple of blocks, but then we got rolling.

"If you feel like you're gonna fall, just say something and we'll stop and start over."

"Okay."

A car full of college kids (I guessed) flashed past on the main road. Hip hop blasted out of the car window. I turned down Winborne. No traffic likely there, as Winborne goes through a neighborhood of small houses. In two blocks, we'd be across the street from Carleton Place. The sky was dark tonight, with big clouds covering the stars and the moon. Occasionally you could see one or two stars when the clouds parted a bit, but the darkness was good for us. Mignon said, "Stop," and I did. She shifted on the bike and got her balance again.

"The hole is by this new building, right across from

the grocery store, on that side of the road. All we need to do is put the Time Box in there and cover it up. Once we get to the construction site you'll have to watch out for the shopping center cops. They cruise around in a white Prius with lights on top. Pretty funny."

"I'm nervous."

"Me, too. Let's go."

I pushed the bike off. Mignon leaned but caught herself as we crossed the main street. Next to the lot where we were heading was a row of abelia plants. They smell good and attract a lot of bees during the day. Fortunately it was night. Those bushes were my target. A pickup truck went by now, creeping along. Somebody in the truck shouted something, but we just kept going. When we reached the abelias, I stopped, Mignon jumped off, and I dumped the bike into the hedge. We waited a minute, looking around.

"The hole is there—where that piece of plywood is, over there," I whispered.

"By that pole?"

"Yeah." I said as I edged up. "You stay here and watch. If you see a car, any car, coming down the road near me or behind you, give a whistle or something and duck down."

"What about a cluck? I can do it. It sounds like a squirrel."

She made that sound and it did sound like an excited squirrel. I wanted to laugh, but didn't.

"Okay."

I didn't see anybody or anything, so I jogged to the hole. I dropped to the ground when I heard the clucks and a car sped past. Then I pulled back the plywood cover and crawled in the hole. I used the light from my phone to look at the bottom. Some water had seeped around the plywood and puddled in the hole. That would make it easier to dig. There was no wire or pipe anywhere. Another couple of clucks, and I ducked deep in the hole. I could hear the car as it revved away. I dug a deeper, smaller hole through the red muck with my spade and set the box solid on the bottom of that hole. This is where it was going to be for a long time so I gave it a long look. It seemed to have a glow, sitting there. Was that my imagination?

I gave the box a pat on the top, to say goodbye. It was tough getting out of the hole, but I pulled myself up and, using my spade, started filling the hole from the pile of red dirt next to it. There was no traffic but the noise of the spade was pretty loud to me. Suddenly, Mignon came running and using just her hands started pushing more dirt into the hole. I was sweating something fierce, both from the work and from nerves. With the two of us working, the hole was getting filled faster.

Then we heard a car noise, and Mignon and I both jumped back behind the construction fence. Scrunching down, we held our breath. A light swept over our heads towards the new building. I could hear country music coming from the car: "Just a kiss on your lips in the moonlight." I peeked around a saved maple tree and saw the white Prius turning the corner and moving away slowly. I waited until I couldn't hear the music anymore. Then I jumped up and started shoveling as fast as I could.

Mignon found a piece of shingle and used that to help. We were both breathing hard, sweat dripping from our faces. It was tough going.

Finally, the hole seemed filled, but I stepped on the mound, packing it in more. I needed more dirt. I found another small pile and scrubbed it over the dips in the hole. Now you could not tell where the hole had been.

Mignon stepped back, hands on her knees. I stopped for a moment, arms aching, and I realized that the Time Box was really buried.

"Let's go!" I said.

We dashed back to the bike and started for home. On the way, the white Prius came towards us and slowed. My heart was pounding. As we passed, the rent-a-cop driver gave me a funny look. I gave him a wave and he smiled, to our relief. He was still listening to Lady Antebellum.

"I thought I was going to pee in my pants the whole time," Mignon said.

"Thanks for coming out there and shoveling."

"I wanted to finish filling the hole quicker—you know, to get it over with, before I fainted or something."

We were flying now, and then I realized. "I forgot my spade."

"Oh, shit," Mignon hissed.

I wheeled the bike around, and we were really moving now. How could I have forgotten that? Stupid. It only took a minute or two to get back to Carleton Place. I wasn't too concerned now about being seen. I jumped off the bike. Mignon held it and I ran to the lot. There it was. I grabbed it and slung it over my shoulder. I rushed back to the bike just in time to see that darn Prius moving forward. He'd been parked in the lot across the street. He must have seen us come back, and now his headlights came on.

I pedaled quickly to Winborne and saw the Prius turn in behind us. He was two or three blocks away when I decided to double back. Follow the follower. It was a strategy in some comic book I remembered. When I was hidden by a dip in the road, I took a right turn down a bumpy street, past a brick apartment building that was in rough shape.

"What now?" Mignon whispered.

"Nothing. We wait for a minute."

A car that could have been the Prius kept going on Winborne, pausing at corners as if it was looking for us. But now we were behind it, and I went back to Winborne. The Prius finally turned on the main road, heading back to the shopping center. They probably couldn't get too far away from Carleton Place. They'd have to call real cops in on the deal. Maybe they had.

With that thought I was really freaked, and got back to the park as fast as I could. We skidded to the picnic table.

"I gotta wash my hands off," I said.

"Me, too," Mignon said.

We went to the creek and dunked our hands in the cool water, washing off the red clay dirt. We tried to dry our hands on some big maple leaves. That didn't work too well, so we both used my jeans for a final wipe-down.

"You'd better get going," I said.

"Yeah. That was pretty exciting." she said, and she was smiling.

"Yeah."

With that, she gave me a cheek kiss and started running. At the streetlight she was going full speed. I pedaled slowly home, dumped the spade by Mom's garden, and eased into the house, leaving my muddy shoes in the hall. I was sneaking up the stairs on my tiptoes when the hall light flicked on. I froze. Suddenly Dad was there on the steps, holding a baseball bat. He studied me for what seemed to be a very long time. My heart was pounding.

"You're lucky I didn't club you," he said.

"Yes, sir." I was wobbly.

"Where you been?" he whispered. His ears had turned bright red.

"Out. Just out. I promise I wasn't doing anything bad. I swear." That was the best I could say.

He stared at me for another long moment. "For now, I'll take your word for it, but that doesn't make it right. No way. If your mother had caught you, you'd be in bigger trouble."

"Yes, sir."

"Don't ever do this again, Tommy. This sneaking out."

"I won't. Never again," I promised.

"You're 12 and still young enough to get a whipping."

"I understand."

"We'll talk about this later. Understand?"

"Yes, sir."

He turned away, and then turned back.

"Did this have something to do with a girl?"

I know I got red in the face. "Sort of."

He nodded and took a deep breath. "Get upstairs and be quiet so you don't wake your Mom and go to bed." I started up the stairs. "And put those filthy jeans in the laundry."

He put the bat down on the landing and went to lock the door. Had he ever snuck out of his house as a kid? I guessed he had.

I dropped those red-clay stained jeans in the laundry room and in a few minutes, I was in my bed and covered up. I took a deep breath and shook myself. I felt proud and relieved. I still might get punished, but the mission was accomplished. My last thought before I fell asleep was of the Time Box, resting peacefully in its new home. Hopefully no one would disturb it for a long, long time.

▪

The next day at school, Mignon and I just looked at each other in the hall. We didn't need to talk about the Time Box. A nod, a smile and a wink said it all. We'd had a secret adventure, and that made us even tighter. At lunch she picked at her food and shook her head.

"You got home okay?" I asked.

"Yeah. My parents are deep sleepers. How about you?"

"It worked out." No need to tell her about Dad.

"I'm so tired. Mental exhaustion," Mignon said with a sigh.

"Me, too."

"I was so scared when we had to go back and the cops

were there and started after us. I thought I was going to have a heart attack."

"It was like a movie chase scene."

"Really. And I can't believe the whole thing actually happened. It's like a dream or something when I think about it."

"Well, it's not over really," I said.

Her face tensed up.

"Until they pave the lot, anything could happen. They could start digging again at something and find the box."

She laughed her nervous laugh. "Don't say that."

"It's true."

"Tommy, you are a bad influence. You think too much."

"Yeah?"

"And then you do stuff."

She was kidding, but she might have been right.

The azaleas in our yard were in full bloom now, and the school days were counting down. The weekend after the Time Box was planted, I went to see Dr. Bugg. Actually, I went to cut his grass one more time as a thank you. He came out when he heard my mower and walked over.

"How you doing?"

"Just want to thank you again," I said.

"Did you get the top on okay?"

"Yes, we did."

"I knew you could do it. Did you get it buried?"

"Yes, sir."

He clapped his hands together. "In a safe place?"

"I hope so."

He gave my shoulder a pat and smiled. "I don't have any cash right now for the yard, but I'm going by the bank later today."

"No, sir. This is free. I wouldn't take any money. This is the only way I know how to thank you."

He rubbed his chin, thinking. "Well, thank you, Thomas. It was a pleasure working with you. A great pleasure."

When he said that, I felt happy, but happy in a serious way, if you know what I mean. That was a great compliment, coming from someone like Dr. Bugg. I restarted the mower as he walked back to the house. Mrs. Bugg was standing at the side door, looking through the screen. She was wearing a big flowery robe. When he opened the door, she put out her hand which he took in his as he led her back inside the dark house.

▪

My Dad kept his word and gave me some punishment for sneaking out. He took away my phone for a few days and then he made me clean up some nasty little parts from the Fiat. I had to put them in a stinky solvent and then brush them with an old toothbrush until they shined. It wasn't so bad except that the smell of the solvent stayed in my nose and on my hands for days. When Mom asked him what was up, he just said, "It's between Tommy and me." That was it.

I biked down to Carleton Place a couple of times after school. Nothing had really changed where the Time Box was buried. Work outside had slowed down a lot. Some new bushes had been planted. One day, an air-conditioning company truck was parked beside the new building; a Franklin Electrical truck was there the next day. That was funny to me, because the name made me think about Ben Franklin standing out in a thunderstorm with a key on a kite waiting for the lightning bolt. That's some real electrical contracting, for sure. Anyway, most of the work was going on inside the new building, or so it seemed to me. But I wouldn't feel safe until the whole lot was paved.

School was pretty much over. We were about a week from the end of the year. The last big deal before I cleaned out my locker was the middle school talent show. Obviously I wasn't on the program. David played bass with his band, the Zipper Kings. Doris Kim played the violin. She was good. Shannon Amounpour did a modern dance which resembled a seizure but really showed how flexible she was. Jacob Meyer played some great piano as expected. Then towards the end of the show, after some juggling by Al Lockhart, Elaine Frish stepped on the stage. Crabby Elaine Frish with her braces gleaming in the spotlight stood knock kneed for a moment while Mrs. Bascombe, the music teacher, got comfortable at the piano. Then a transformation happened. That's all I can call it. Elaine opened her mouth and out came this amazing voice singing Adele's "One an Only". I was blown away. Mignon gave me the "I told you so" look. Smiles covered both of our faces. On the stage, with her eyes closed and her body rocking to the rhythm of the song, she became a different, stronger person. A parent next to me started crying. Even I had a shiver. When she stopped singing there was a moment of complete silence and then the audience burst into cheering and clapping. A few guys called out her name. Elaine gave a little bow and suddenly the old shy, suspicious Elaine returned. Her body seemed to coil up as she tiptoed off the stage almost tripping on the last step. You never know what's inside a person. That was a great lesson.

Everybody had pretty much planned their summers. I was still thinking about the Methodist camp, but knew we might be too late now to register. What I really wanted to do was stay close to home, and Mignon. I needed to talk to her about that. She hadn't said anything about what she was planning for the summer. Her friend Jeannie was heading to a beach camp before going to the mountains with her parents. That was good. And her other best friend, Brenda, was visiting her grandparents for three or four weeks. So Mignon and I would have plenty of time just to hang out together. We could rent a boat out on Lake Waverly and sail around. We could do some hiking in Umstead Park. We could even bike around the city on the Greenway. We both liked to swim. Pools would be open soon. I could write another story and she could illustrate it. This was my thinking, or dreaming.

After school, Mignon and I would still walk home together. Kareem only joined us every now and then. He had grown another inch or two and would stay at school with some other basketball players most days, so he could work out and do drills in the gym.

Mignon and I never talked about the Time Box. It was our secret and somehow we were happy to keep it that way. If we had told somebody, like Micky or Jeannie, they really wouldn't have understood the whole thing, unless I started telling them how and why I wanted to make the box. Even then, I don't think they would really get it.

Sometimes, when Mignon and I were walking by ourselves and the weather was good, we'd take a long way home, cutting through the old Double-A cemetery that we'd visited months before. When we did, we'd pick up any trash we saw and put it in the dumpster, because we remembered the old man and what he said.

On this day, we found a lot of trash: McDonald's bags and cups, a Chick-Fil-A box, and one white sock.

"You know what?" I asked Mignon. Understand, people ask this question all the time. So you say, "Do you know what?" and, of course, the person doesn't know "what" and is supposed to say, "No," and then you have the right to tell him or her the "what." It's a dumb question, but everybody uses it. So I waited for her to answer.

"Yes," she said.

"You do?"

"Yeah."

"You can't!" I said.

"Sure I can," she said.

"Screw you!"

We both laughed.

"Okay, Tommy, what?"

"Well, we both like each other, right?"

"Duh."

She seemed slightly irritated, I thought. Why had I started this? "Summer's coming, with lots of stuff to do."

That was pretty obvious.

"Yeah." She nodded. "So what's the point?"

"I was thinking that maybe we could sort of let it be known that we're boyfriend and girlfriend—like, official."

The minute I said it, I was having second thoughts. She dropped some trash in the dumpster and gave me a sideways look.

"Why?" she asked.

"I don't know. I think it would be good to let other people know, you know, the situation."

"People...know we like each other. We spend a lot of time together. Everybody we know knows that." Now she seemed really irritated. "People don't care. You care. Why can't you say that?" she asked.

Suddenly I felt very stupid.

"It's just a thought. Can I take it back?" I was searching for a way out.

"No. You have to have had a reason to ask something like that."

"I just feel a little uneasy, like nervous, for some crazy reason. Maybe I need a little...I can't think of the word."

"That would be the first time. You have a big vocabulary."

I was struggling. Mignon looked up in the sky. "There's a hawk. A red tail." she said. The hawk made a circle and then swooped down among the treetops and became a blur. Mignon watched him all the way. "He's hunting," she said.

I was hunting, too—for the right words. I took a big breath.

"Look, sometimes I wonder if you really care about me because lately, you've been...."

"Then you're pretty stupid," she interrupted. "Why would I spend all this time with you? Why do we talk almost every night?" She was right, but why was she so angry?

"You're right. I just get into a weird mood or something. I just worry."

"You worry about a lot of things, Tommy."

"I do. I wish I didn't."

"And what's summer got to do with it?" she asked.

"Well, we'll be out of school, so we won't see each other every day, like, automatically. We'll have to think about getting together. Make plans. Micky—he invited us down to the beach. They rent a house there every summer."

Her face didn't look very happy. She stared at the ground.

"Oh, the hell with it. I'm sorry I brought it up. Can we forget it?" I felt dumb; clumsy. Mignon sighed but didn't speak.

"Okay, let's get home," I said.

She nodded, and just as I picked up my backpack, she came close and pulled me around. She hesitated as if she wanted to say something but, biting her lip, she grabbed her backpack and headed out of the cemetery in a trot.

"Hey. What's the hurry?"

She wasn't running, but her strides were long and I had trouble keeping up with her.

"I'm sorry. Can't you say something? What's the

matter?"

Suddenly she turned and stopped. Her eyes were shining.

"I'm leaving this summer. We're moving back to Louisiana. Dad got a new job and we're going back to Baton Rouge at the end of June."

There was an awful silence. I felt like someone had punched me in my chest. Her face was hard but tears welled up in her eyes. She started walking again, and when we reached our park, she plopped down on a picnic bench and wiped her eyes.

"When did you find out?" I asked.

"For real? Yesterday. But Dad told me he was thinking about it months ago."

"What'd you say?"

"I said I didn't want to go, but I don't have much choice. It's a good new job. We have family down there. I'm 12. My vote's not really important. So what good would it have been if I was your girlfriend for the summer? Tell me, what good?"

I couldn't look at her. I felt sick to my stomach.

"This is awful," I said.

She shook her head. "How do you think I feel? It's me that's leaving." More tears on her pale cheeks. I wanted to say something that would make her feel better.

"Damn," is all I could manage.

"Double damn," she muttered into her hands that cupped her face.

I just wanted to break something.

The spring sun was setting later now and the light was

finding it hard to get through the new leaves. Mignon's sad face was partly in light and partly in shadow.

"Maybe, you should look for a new girlfriend; use the summer to find somebody for next year. I know Brenda likes you, and that new girl, Samantha, she's very pretty."

"Shut up!" I shouted.

Mignon jumped up from the bench and ran towards home. I didn't chase her. I stayed in the park for a while, trying to calm down. I waited for the sun to touch the overpass bridge and start setting behind it. I was sadder than I had ever been.

CHAPTER EIGHTEEN

THAT NIGHT, MOM noticed I hardly ate, but she didn't say much about it. I went to my room and lay on the bed, staring at the ceiling. I felt empty. The universe was lonely enough without this happening. I tried calling Mignon, but she didn't answer. She was probably too upset to talk. To be honest, she was my first real girlfriend. The first girl who ever really kissed me by her own free will, and now she was going to Baton Rouge.

What kind of name for a town was that? I went to my computer and googled it. The name means red stick. Some French explorer discovered a bloody stick dug in the ground. It was a border mark for the local Indians. That's how the name got started and surprisingly, it hung on. Crazy.

The city is on the Mississippi. I couldn't help but think about Huck Finn and Tom Sawyer, whose adventures I'd read about last year. It might as well have been Paris or Moscow to me. It was a long way away. Almost 1,000 miles from here. One thousand miles was better than 100 million light years, but not by much, considering my mode of travel—a two-year-old Trek bike. I buried my head in my pillow, and all I could feel was that anger, that sad anger. The feeling was like when I heard that Uncle Aaron had died. There was nothing you could do to change what happened. Nothing.

■

Sadness makes everything different. The next morning, I didn't want to get out of bed. I didn't want to go to school. Mom pushed my door open.

"Tommy, I don't know what's happened and you don't have to tell me. But I do know that sitting in the dark, in your room, feeling down is not going to solve anything or make you feel any better. So get up and get out in the sunlight."

There was something in her calm voice that always got to me.

"Could you toast me up a couple of Eggos?" I asked.

She nodded and I swung my legs to the floor. It was going to be a tough day.

Let's get right to it. Mignon saw me walking up the hall, and she looked like she wanted to run. But she stood, legs apart and little jittery, until I got close.

"Sorry about yesterday," I said.

"Me, too," she said.

And then I walked away, because I had nothing else to say. I had nothing to say, because if I had started talking, I would have had too much to say. I was a zombie moving through the school day. Micky ambled up. He's always up and positive. That day, it was annoying.

"You got to come to the beach. It'll be so much fun."

"I don't want to talk about it."

He was surprised. "Okay, my bad."

"Look, I don't know about anything really, right now."

"Whoa. You and Mignon—something going on there?"

How had he picked that up? I wanted to punch him, and then I wanted to tell him. I did neither one and headed to science class.

Lunch was a mess. I looked at the lame, pitiful hot dog and knew if I ate it I would taste it the rest of the afternoon. So I put hot sauce and mustard and whatever else I could find on it. Then I chomped it down like a punishment.

Jeannie came over. "She just told me she's leaving. I can't believe it. She's devastated. You can't be mean to her."

"I'm not mean to her."

"When you don't talk to her, that's mean," Jeannie said, looking me straight in the face.

As much as Jeannie normally annoyed me, she was right this time. I found Mignon in the corner of the cafeteria, with Elaine and Brenda. They both left when I walked up.

"Are you okay?" I asked.

"Sort of. You?"

"Frankly, I embarrass myself. I'm a mess, but we need to talk this out."

She finally smiled. "Meet you in the park?"

"Yeah."

My zombie march ended with the last bell. I went home and rode to the park after dinner. Mignon was waiting when I got there.

"My dad is so mad at me. I yelled at him yesterday. Kind of a tantrum, I guess."

"It's made me feel right sick, to be honest," I said.

"Someday we'll be able to follow our feelings. Someday." A little too Taylor Swift for her. She made a face like she understood how she sounded. "Sorry. Such b.s."

"Well, I've been thinking about this as much as I can stand. We're not dissolving. We still can text and Facetime. Instagram. We can keep in touch."

"You think?" she asked, with a half-smile.

"Yeah. And maybe you can come back here some time. Stay with Jeannie or Brenda. Or maybe I can come down to Baton Rouge."

"That would be funny to see you there."

"Maybe I'd come floating down the river on my raft, like Huck Finn." I was just half joking.

"Yeah. I can picture it. How old was Huck Finn?"

"Twelve, thirteen. I looked it up."

She laughed. "You would look it up."

Suddenly, and without warning, I was feeling better, just being with her again. "Look, we got the Time Box buried. That was a big deal for me, and you're a real part of that. Couldn't have done it without you. That's the honest truth and you know it." I was hunting for the words. "We've done a lot of stuff together and we've got some time to do more, so let's not waste it feeling bad."

She punched me softly. "Are you still angry?" she asked.

"No, I'm sad. Aren't you a little sad?"

"Yeah. You're my best friend. That's it."

When I looked up, I saw tears in her eyes and they were starting in mine. And for whatever reason, we both started laughing at how sad we were.

▪

School ended, with the usual yelling and jumping at the last bell. Girls hugged. Boys fist-pumped. Yearbooks were signed with promises and jokes. After that Mignon and I had more time together. We went hiking. We went to the movies. We tried to play tennis in the park. The pool had opened right as school ended, and Mignon and I hung out there on the warmest days. We would float together at the deep end, holding hands as we sank to the bottom, holding our breaths until we had to rise or drown. We would rise at the last second, breaking the surface, gasping for air.

We went to Lake Waverly to rent a boat, like we'd talked about. We had the idea that we could sail all day around the shoreline. Just drifting.

"How old are you, bud?" a red-headed guy behind the counter asked. He had a big pimple on his neck.

"I'll be thirteen soon."

He pointed to a sign behind him on the wall. "Got to be sixteen to rent any kind of boat out here. Sorry."

As usual, we were too young. We walked around the

lake and down to the stream that fed it. At about two o'clock, it started raining like crazy and we ran back towards the boat house. We hid in one of the shelters while the thunder boomed and the lightning lit up the sky. We were soaked. That's when I kissed her myself, not waiting for her. Not waiting for her to give permission. And then she kissed me back and leaned into my arms while we watched the lightning flash over the lake. We stayed for a few more minutes, until her dad came and rescued us from the storm. I wondered if he could tell what we were up to, or if he could see how happy we were in that moment. That's how the final days played out. Then, suddenly, it was deep June.

We hadn't talked much about the move or exactly how it worked. In fact, we didn't say much at all. We just hung out together. Face time for real.

"Tomorrow the trucks are loading our stuff," she said.

"Yeah?" There was a lump in my throat.

"They'll take the furniture and the big stuff and we're driving the Suburban."

"What happened to your mom's car?"

"We sold it at CarMax."

"Do you need any help packing up?"

"I don't think so. We sleep in our beds tonight and then the movers pack those up."

"I'll come over to say goodbye."

"You better."

"When's a good time?"

"Around lunch. That's when Dad says we're starting out. I don't think we'll make it the first day. We'll stop somewhere."

"It's a long trip."

She nodded. "We could make it in one day, but Mom said we should take it easy."

I could hear her mom calling for her in the background.

"I'll see you tomorrow."

"Okay."

That afternoon, I helped Dad pull the seats out of the Fiat. They seemed in pretty good shape, but he wanted to get to the dashboard easier. I thought the work would keep my mind from wandering. It didn't. We had fish for dinner. Our neighbor had caught some blues at the beach and gave us a couple.

"You did a good job in school this year, Tommy. Keep it up," Dad said.

"How about me?" asked Ella, putting in her two cents' worth.

"You too, sport. You did good. But you had that talking in class problem."

"People were talking to me, not me to them."

"Whatever," Dad said.

I went to bed early and tried to think of what I could give Mignon as a going away present. I didn't want to be too mushy. Flowers would just die on the road. Something funny would be good. I could have used that Sponge Bob I put in the Time Box. Maybe stuff like that didn't matter. That's when I found it, stuffed in the corner of my desk drawer. Just a token. That's it.

Around eleven o'clock, I went over to her house. A big

truck was there and the workers were loading the beds. The Suburban was in the driveway. Thankfully, Pierre was already in the truck. Mrs. Eubanks gave me a smile. She was packing a few things in a box on the lawn. There was a For Sale sign right by the sidewalk.

"Mignon's inside, seeing if she's left anything."

I went inside the house, which now looked really big without all the furniture in the rooms.

"Hey, Mignon," I called.

"I'm downstairs," she yelled.

I hurried down to the basement den. Mignon was looking through the shelves. The old paint-spattered boom box was sitting on the floor.

"How you doing?" I asked.

"Okay."

"Looks like you guys are ready to go."

"Soon."

She just stood there and I stood there, as well. We looked at each other and we both felt, I guess, helpless.

"I found you a little going-away present," I said.

"You didn't have to do that."

"Don't get excited. It's not much." I pulled the medallion from my pocket. "I went to Carowinds a couple of years ago and just made up this good luck coin in a machine. You put your name on it and a birth date or special message or something. Four-leaf clover in the middle. I carried it with me all the time. I thought it would give me good luck. Proved to be."

"How?" she asked.

"I met you."

Another pause.

"Maybe it should have been in the box," Mignon said.

"Well, good luck pieces are no good buried in a box. But maybe it'll be good luck for you."

She held the medallion, studied it. "Thanks. I'll need it." She put it in the back pocket of her shorts. "But I don't have anything for you."

"You're the one who's leaving."

"Yes, I am." She put some old magazines in a plastic trashcan.

"You leaving the boom box?" I asked.

"Yeah. Nobody uses it anymore. You can have it if you want."

"Nah."

"Not even for sentimental reasons?"

She picked up the boom box and opened it. "It's still got the CD in it that we danced to."

The memory of that afternoon came back in my head. It seemed a hundred years ago. "Well, I wouldn't mind another dance lesson, so I don't forget how to do it."

"Sure," she said with a smile.

Honestly, I just wanted to hold her one more time. She plugged in the boom box and pushed play. The music was loud in this empty, silent room. She came close. "Ready?"

"Yep."

She took my hand and I held her waist. Soon we were dancing easy to that sad, slow song but truly, my heart was hurting. That's the only way I can describe that feeling. The big ache. My hand trembled in her hand. Up to this moment we had been so normal, so calm. Then Mignon started to cry softly and buried her head in my shoulder. But we kept shuffling. Her crying made me start to cry, too. I couldn't dance anymore. We stopped, our arms wrapped around each other. Mignon shook, she was crying so hard.

"I'll never forget you, Tommy. Never. I promise."

"And I'll never forget you, either."

"I love you," Mignon whispered.

"I love you, too."

"I'm sorry," she said.

"For what?" I asked, but she didn't answer.

I held her and I thought, is there anything greater under this big, expanding, impossible to measure universe than this feeling we have for each other, down here in the basement? Is there anything crazier than that? We're somewhere between the speed of light and the darkness of those old graves.

"Mignon!" her dad called.

And that was it. We wiped off our tears on our sleeves. I shook hands with Mr. Eubanks and got a hug from Mrs. Eubanks. The big truck had already left and now the Suburban cranked up. Mignon got in the back seat with Pierre. The car was totally full. They even had stuff strapped to the top, covered by a tarp. Mignon gave me a sad wave and then, just like that, she was gone.

The night after Mignon left, the moon was enormous—so large and bright that the stars around it were dim. On the news, they said this was the time of year when the moon comes closest to Earth. Standing in my yard in its yellow light, I wondered if Mignon was seeing and feeling it, too.

The next week went by in kind of a dream. I was able to get registered for the Methodist camp in late July. That should be two weeks of fun. I saw Micky and David a couple of times. I was trying to warm them to the idea of adding Sean Mac, as we called him, to our informal group.

"For a Yankee, he's a good guy," Micky said.

I laughed out loud. "Coming from you, that's hysterical."

I started running on the greenway and in town. That let me keep an eye on the bank parking lot. I talked to Mignon's friend, Elaine, and Jeannie, too. I think there's a chance I can become good friends with Jeannie, maybe because she feels hurt too. Maybe I misjudged her.

Anyway, Mignon and I have kept in touch over the weeks. At first, it was hard to text or even email. I didn't know what to say or what to ask. Now we Facetime often, but not as often as we did before. It's hard to talk about what you're doing with other people, when the person you spent the most time with is gone.

I went over to Carleton Place again. I could smell the asphalt before I got there. I rushed to the lot. They were paving. I watched until they were done. That was great. I took a photo as they lined the asphalt and then I was able to add an arrow pointing to where the Time Box was buried. I sent it to Mignon. She seemed very happy to know the box was safe.

Ever since the paving was completed, I've felt calm. I don't know how to explain it, but somehow, having that box in the ground and paved over has made me not worry so much, even about the endless stars and the black holes sucking up the light. I'm sad and I miss Mignon. But what can you do?

For her part, Mignon tries to tell me how things are there and how she's fitting in with the new people and places. Not much to know yet until the new school year starts, but the family plans to go down to the Gulf in Mississippi for some swimming about the time I'm in camp. And frankly, I feel our friendship changing a little, and the changing adds to the ache, if you know what I mean. All the Facetime is different when you never see the person in school or at home or in the park. I think what we had was real important. It was love. That's all you can call it. It would be nice to think that those feelings could last forever, but only time will tell if we can keep a grip on each other.

▪

Last week, Mignon sent me a photo of herself, standing by the Mississippi River. She was dressed in her yellow shorts and her familiar sandals. She was shading her eyes with her left hand and her right hand was on her hip as she stared down the river. She wrote a caption for the photo. It said: "At the Mississippi, waiting for the raft. I miss you still."

That's where I have to leave it.

Thanks to
Rachel McKay, Carrie Knowles,
Sylvia Wilkinson, Laura DeVivo,
Charles Nemes, Sylvie Rabineau,
David Freeman, Steve Kloves
and Karin Fremer

lcapetanos.com